The Haiku Apprentice

The Haiku Apprentice

MEMOIRS OF WRITING
POETRY IN JAPAN

Abigail Friedman

Foreword by Michael Dylan Welch

Stone Bridge Press • Berkeley, California

Published by
Stone Bridge Press
P. O. Box 8208
Berkeley, California 94707
www.stonebridge.com • sbp@stonebridge.com

LIBRARY OF CONGRESS CATALOGING-IN-PUBLICATION DATA
Friedman, Abigail.
   The haiku apprentice: memoirs of writing poetry in Japan / Abigail
Friedman.
   p. cm.
   ISBN-13: 978-1-933330-04-4
   ISBN-10: 1-933330-04-X
   Includes bibliographical references (p.).
   1. Haiku—Authorship. 2. Friedman, Abigail. 3. Poets, American—20th
century—Biography. I. Title.
   PN1525.F75 2006
   808.1′41—DC22
                 2005037613

CONTENTS

part 1   珍しさ   *Mezurashisa*
THE EXTRAORDINARY

part 2   友愛   *Yūai*
FELLOWSHIP

part 3   調和 *Chōwa*

HARMONY

FOREWORD: A DEEPER ATTENTION

Everywhere, ordinary people are writing haiku. An American soldier in Iraq, a retiree in Scotland, a South African housewife. A daycare worker in British Columbia, a California psychologist, a technical writer in New York. These are just a few examples of adults who compose haiku regularly. What's more, English-speaking children nearly always learn haiku in school. Haiku has for some time been the world's most popular genre of poetry—not only because it's quick to write and quick to read, but because it serves as a simple poetic outlet for everyday experience that everyone can relate to.

The immediacy and accessibility of this poetry can be deceptive, however, for haiku is very challenging to write well. French philosopher Roland Barthes once wrote that "haiku has this rather fantasmagorical property: that we always suppose we ourselves can write such things easily." While haiku is easy to write, dedicated poets still spend lifetimes exploring the depths of its history and aesthetics. They study such key techniques as the use of a *kigo*, or season word, that anchors the poem in time and alludes to other poems, and of a *kireji*, or cutting word, that typically divides the poem and engages readers in intuiting the relationship between its two juxtaposed parts.

In Japan, an estimated seven to ten million people write haiku every month. All who write literary haiku—both ordinary people and professional poets around the world—share a desire to write with simplicity and empathy, to write authentically of their personal experiences, whatever those experiences might be. The tone and content of haiku can vary from wonder and joy to melancholy and sadness, with both authors and readers appreciating life in all its phases, not merely the beautiful. Typically, the poet dwells on the details of seasonal and human events in order to represent and celebrate the ordinary and everyday, thereby making it extraordinary.

In the gently unfolding memoir that follows, American diplomat Abigail Friedman tells the story of her first encounter with a Japanese haiku group and how she began to learn the aesthetics of this centuries-old poetic genre. Her diplomatic work in Japan charged her with coordinating the U.S. and Japanese approaches to North Korea, to improve the situation especially regarding the nuclear threat and human rights. With haiku she learned to describe experience without an agenda to change anything. While she found haiku writing relaxing, she also discovered an important similarity between the poem's careful objective description and her own work as a diplomat: both are concerned with truly understanding and describing things as they are.

Haiku proved to be a useful part of Abigail's modern, busy, care-worn life. Though not previously a poet, she fell under haiku's spell, dipping her toe, and then her foot, into its captivating pond. Under the tutelage of Kuroda Momoko, the sensei or "master" of the Aoi haiku group, she learned not just the aesthetics of haiku but the aesthetics and values of traditional yet modern Japanese culture. Abigail learned that, just as she herself was a professional diplomat, haiku poets come from all walks of life, and that this very richness of experience helps make haiku captivating.

Kuroda-sensei, it should be noted, is one of Japan's foremost haiku masters and a leading member of Japan's Haiku Poet's Association. Born in 1938, and once a student of Yamaguchi Seison, she declined an offer to succeed Yamaguchi as leader of the Natsukusa (Summer Grass) haiku group, proposing, in deference to her master, that the group's name be retired to honor him. She then formed her own group and called it Aoi (Indigo). Kuroda-sensei has published many haiku books and books about haiku, including well-respected *saijiki* (season-word almanacs). She also appears on haiku television shows and judges major Japanese haiku contests. While many hundreds of haiku groups in Japan are led by prominent haiku masters, Kuroda-sensei is among the more esteemed, giving the narrative here added import. Yet, as you will see, Abigail's story and the people in it retain an unpretentious humility and a respect for tradition even as tradition is modernized in contemporary society.

This book, with its focus on the traditional poetic art of haiku, reveals both Japan and the author's life in the context of modern stresses—both political and personal. Yet it shows how haiku can be a rewarding addition to anyone's life, not just the life of Abigail Friedman. In Japan, one encounters haiku in hotel lobbies, in restaurants, in roadside shrines, and in most daily newspapers. While haiku is not as ubiquitous outside Japan, this engaging memoir clarifies why that situation is changing, and it explains how haiku can be a meaningful part of your life, whether you consider yourself a writer or not.

This is a book for poets and nonpoets, for the culturally curious, for those who have visited Japan and those who would like to. This is a book for those seeking an antidote for the assaults of modern life; it is for those who also recognize that global awareness can have tremendous value in our changing world, and that all of life rewards our close attention. Turn the page and join Abigail Friedman on her journey into the haiku poetry of contemporary Japan, a poetry rich with awareness and wonder that cannot help but bring us to deeper attention.

MICHAEL DYLAN WELCH
Vice President, Haiku Society of America
Sammamish, Washington

ACKNOWLEDGMENTS

This book could not have been written without the warm support of Kuroda Momoko and members of the Numamomo and Aoi haiku groups. Individuals belonging to these groups, and especially Kuroda Momoko herself, gave of themselves freely in conversations and interviews over many months. I thank them for their kindness and their confidence in my work.

Many people contributed to the making of this book. I never would have given haiku a second thought had I not met Elizabeth Guinsbourg in Paris and, during the course of our friendship, learned that she writes haiku. Janine Beichman kept me going when I first started writing this book, with one simple word of encouragement, *Avanti!* Bill Higginson, Miyashita Emiko, and Michael Dylan Welch, three wonderful teachers whom I feel honored to call friends, helped me across the finish line. I also want to thank the many members of the Haiku Society of America and Haiku North America who introduced me to contemporary American haiku when I returned to the United States and gave me good advice on starting haiku groups. Janine Beichman, John Dickson, Peter Folejewski, John Gribble, Elizabeth Guinsbourg, Bill Higginson, Danielle Michelman, Miyashita Emiko, Mizuniwa Susumu, Nakamura Kuniko, Eric Passaglia, Marianna Pierce, Ueki Katsumi, and Michael Dylan Welch each read through some or all of the text and gave me helpful feedback.

My initial translations of the haiku in this book proved to be only a crude beginning. I owe a special debt of gratitude to poet and author Arthur Binard, who contributed his poetic talent to many of these translations, preserving the wit and beauty of the original Japanese text. At a later stage in the process, Bill Higginson made sure my translations were consistent with American haiku usage. I must confess to a stubborn streak, and I did not always follow their wise counsel. Any infelicities in the haiku translations are my own.

Every author needs a good editor, mentor, and advisor. John Gribble took on this thankless task, sticking by my endeavor and offering sound counsel, especially during those many times that I declared the manuscript and myself hopeless. Without John's help, this book would not now be in your hands. After Stone Bridge Press accepted my manuscript, Elizabeth Floyd took over the editing process. Working with someone of her talent and integrity has been a pleasure.

Over time, writers become incredibly boring, distracted souls. I am infinitely grateful for the love of my husband, Eric Passaglia, and our children, Abraham, Martha, and Samuel. It has been a long journey, much longer than any of us anticipated, and I thank my family for their grace, understanding, and humor.

A.F.

NOTES ON THE TEXT

The events and people I describe in this memoir are real. The events took place over a two-year period in Japan. For the sake of the flow of the narrative, I have condensed the events and conversations into a one-year time frame. On matters of foreign policy, the opinions and views I express in this book are my own and do not necessarily represent the official views of the Department of State or the U.S. Government.

A word on Japanese pronunciation: Japanese vowels are pronounced as in Spanish: *a, i, u, e, o*. In haiku, the beat of each word is important to counting syllables. Spoken Japanese sounds very regular because each syllable is one beat. Some vowel sounds are lengthened and held for two beats; this is indicated by a macron over the vowel, as in *ō*. Where the Japanese reading would consist of two *o*'s, this also is indicated by a macron. A regular *o* counts as one syllable, while *ō* counts as two. One other point to note about counting syllables in Japanese is that the letter *n*, when it comes at the end of a word or at the close of a syllable, is a single syllable in itself. So the word *mon*, or "gate," is actually two syllables: *mo-n*.

In rendering Japanese names into roman script, I have followed Japanese custom of giving the family name first.

All the translations of haiku are mine, unless otherwise stated.

1

珍しさ

mezurashisa

THE EXTRAORDINARY

one

THE MAN FROM HIROSHIMA

It was a man from Hiroshima with a Buddha-like smile who introduced me to haiku in Japan. Thinking back, there was little else that distinguished him. He was about sixty-five years old, bald, and of middling height. He wore a polo shirt, polyester pants, and loafers—much like a golfer, which he later told me he was.

I had just finished giving a presentation on the topic of Northeast Asia to a group of about twenty elderly Bunkyo University alumni and their friends gathered in a midsize hotel in downtown Tokyo. As an American diplomat in Japan, I spent many evenings talking to informal groups like this one about world events and especially about North Korea, whose worrisome missiles and nuclear ambitions were front-page news in Japan.

It was late, and I was tired. I sensed my audience did not care what I said; they were of a generation where a foreigner speaking Japanese was enough to grab their attention.

Still, the evening was far from over. Nearly every occasion in Japan requires a brief *aisatsu*, a mixture of a toast and self-introduction, and I knew tonight would be no different. I had not thought about what I would say. Giving a speech in Japanese was hard enough. Although I had lived in Japan for nearly eight years spread over two decades and had spent a good ten years learning the language, I had still devoted the better part of a month preparing for this speech. I wrote a draft in English and had it translated, then asked a Japanese colleague to read it into a tape recorder. I carried the tape around with me for days, earphones on, tape recorder running, mumbling aloud as I pushed my way through the crowded streets of Tokyo. The previous Saturday afternoon I practiced the speech while sitting on the sidelines of my nine-year-old son Sam's soccer practice, mouthing the phrases, pausing the tape now and again to look a word up in the dictionary. At one point, Sam came over to tell me his team was switching fields and that I had to move. Later, his foot appeared on the ground in front of me. I looked up at him as from a fog. *Mom, tie my shoe*, he instructed gently. I stopped the tape and tied his shoe, wondering as I did so whether my failure to run up and down the field cheering him on would make him a less confident adult. I finished tying his shoe and kissed his chubby leg. He ran back onto the field, and my uncertainty evaporated in the crisp fall air as the distance between us grew.

People were getting up from their chairs, and heading out. I followed them into the room next door, where there were several buffet tables, seats along the back wall, and a standing microphone in the center. I took a seat and looked at my watch. It was 9:30 P.M. By now our three children would be in bed and my husband would be quietly reading. I had missed another evening with my family. What was I doing in this hotel among strangers? Someone was at the microphone. It was hard to tune into his Japanese mid-course. I listened to his voice without hearing the words, a waterfall of sounds splashing in no predictable direction.

We were on the tenth floor of the hotel. My thoughts drifted. What would happen if an earthquake hit right at that moment? I thought I might be feeling some tremors. Earthquakes are common in Japan. At home we had moved all the bookcases away from the beds and we kept a half-dozen gallon jugs of water under the kitchen sink in case the water supply became contaminated. I tried to size up the strength of the beams facing me. If there were an earthquake right now, would it be better for me to hug the vertical beams or run to the door frame? Everyone in Japan is told to run to the door frame; I would use my wits and go for the beam. People would be shrieking and shouting. Sirens would be going off. A woman would grab her purse and then drop it when she realized her survival was all that mattered. I imagined myself crouching behind the beam, protected from flying shards of glass. I would spring into action—cool, levelheaded, reassuring people and directing them to safety. If it was a really big earthquake, I would call the State Department Operations Center in Washington from my cell phone: the first to report it, our woman in Tokyo.

The bald man in the polo shirt came to sit in the empty seat next to me, and I floated back to reality, mechanically reaching for my business cards. As a professional woman in Japan, I had learned to get my *meishi*, or business cards, across early, not just because women are often underestimated in Japan, but because of an important corollary: rank trumps gender. Once they saw I was a diplomat, I came to life for my interlocutors.

I kept my *meishi* in a neat leather holder; his were jammed in his billfold. He spent a few moments searching through his wallet, slowly pulling out and replacing a few until he found the one with his own name on it:

Ōiwa Kōhei

Numamomo Haiku Group

Haiku name: Ryojinboku

This was a very odd Japanese calling card. Mr. Ōiwa had no company affiliation. What was the Numamomo Haiku Group? Did Mr. Ōiwa work there? And if so, what was his position? I knew a little about haiku, those unrhymed Japanese poems capturing the essence of a moment, usually seventeen syllables in Japanese. I liked reading haiku at night before going to bed. They were short and quick to read, and I was a busy person. I liked being able to read a beautiful haiku for relaxation while at the same time improving my Japanese-language skills.

The man also seemed to have two names. Should I refer to him as Mr. Ōiwa or as Mr. Ryojinboku? I was not sure what Ryojinboku meant, although I could see that the three characters—旅、人、木—individually stood for Traveling Man Tree. I pictured Mr. Ōiwa as a man-tree with a kind smile and warm eyes, with leafy branches delicately growing from his head as he walked, dragging roots at his feet and stopping occasionally to rest and compose haiku.

On the reverse side of his business card, Traveling Man Tree had carefully listed his interests and affiliations:

Hiroshima A-bomb Survivors Association

Nikko Securities Friendship Association, Board of Directors

Yuzawa Golf Club, Board of Directors

Hachioji Country Club, Food Committee Chair

Numazu Tasters' Association, Chairman

Oshidori Association (Yuzawa Country Club)

New Century Club, Member

Numazu Cultural Chat Club, Member

Hiroshima A-bomb Survivors Association. My husband and I had lived in Hiroshima for nearly two years shortly after we were married. It was our first experience living in Japan. My husband, an English teacher, had grown up in a Navy family reading books on World War II, watching samurai movies, and dreaming of Japan. When he was offered a job in Hiroshima, it was a chance for him to see with his own eyes a place that for years had lived in his imagination. As for me, Japan held no special meaning, but neither did my job as a lawyer in Washington, D.C. Within a month of his job offer, I closed my fledgling solo practice, said goodbye to family and friends, and left with him for the land of the rising sun. I was one month pregnant.

Eight months later I was in labor on the third floor of Dr. Takahara's Lady Clinic, desperately trying to convey in broken Japanese, *May I now have the honorable injection please?* (The injection never came and this is when I first learned the importance of speaking the language of the country where I live.)

I looked at Traveling Man Tree's card again. I could have met Traveling Man Tree at the time I was living in Hiroshima, without even realizing it, but back then he would have been just another faceless, middle-aged businessman to me. My Japanese was so poor that it would have been impossible for me to strike up a conversation with a stranger anyway. It was only some months after settling in Hiroshima that I began studying Japanese. My husband and I were living in a tiny Japanese-style apartment. Each day as he left for work, I would hear the frosted-glass sliding door rattle shut and wonder how I was going to find a job in a country where I did not speak the language, where my American law degree meant nothing, and where no one would hire a visibly pregnant woman. To pass the time, I signed up for Japanese classes at the local YWCA. This is how I started learning Japanese, and for the next fifteen years I never stopped.

Hiroshima A-bomb Survivors Association. I had never met an A-bomb survivor face-to-face. I wanted to ask Traveling Man Tree about his experience, but I did not dare. How does one begin such a conversation? I hesitated, then decided that perhaps haiku would be a better conversation opener.

After all, it had never occurred to me while reading Japanese haiku in bed at night that I might meet someone in Japan who actually wrote haiku. In my mind, Japanese haiku poets were either long dead or living somewhere hidden away in the hills, practicing Zen in a Buddhist monastery. I had imagined haiku poets in long, flowing robes, writing haiku with an ink brush on an elegant scroll. I looked at Traveling Man Tree, in his polyester pants and polo shirt. He nodded to me kindly, unaware of my thoughts.

I would love to hear more about your hobby, I said in my best Japanese.

Golf! It's a wonderful hobby, I've been enjoying it for more than forty years, he answered. I was confused. If golf was his hobby, then what role did haiku play in his life? Could it be his profession?

Excuse me. I thought haiku was your hobby.

Oh no. Golf is my hobby. I do haiku, he answered, with no apparent intention to confuse.

I considered dropping the subject entirely, but decided to make one last run at it. *Well, how would you compare haiku to golf?*

This question made sense to Traveling Man Tree and he answered:

When I was working at Nikko Securities, before I retired, my hours were very long. Often I had to leave for the office at seven in the morning, and I would not get back home until eleven at night. That was what it was like in those days in Japan, in the 1970s and 1980s—working all the time. Even when I was that busy though, I still had the energy to go out on Sundays and play golf. Lots of people were surprised that I could golf as well as I did after working so hard during the week. Most people, you know, just took pills and slept all weekend to recover. But I played golf—and when I did, I forgot about work, I forgot about my troubles.

I'm not saying that playing golf is an escape, mind you. Golf isn't about running away from work. It's just that golf can change my mood. It's also a matter of concentration. If you don't concentrate when you play golf, your game won't go very well. With both work and golf, concentration is important.

Haiku is different. For me, haiku is a question of feeling, of sensibility. I can't just work sixteen-hour days and then say to myself, "Okay, if I concentrate hard, if I work at finding just the right word, I will compose a good haiku." I need to change how I approach the world. I need to look at the flowers and the grass beside the road. I've got to try to write poetry about what I see around me. I believe that the more I approach haiku in this way and the more I understand the essence of haiku, the better my poetry will be.

I asked Traveling Man Tree if he would show me one of his haiku. He dug into his pocket and pulled out a wrinkled piece of paper. Smoothing it out on his knee, he wrote:

潮風をたもとにいれて吊るしびな
shiokaze o tamoto ni irete tsurushi bina

a sea breeze
billowing in the sleeve
of hanging dolls

I wrote this haiku during the Doll Festival in March. My wife and I had gone to the baths at Inatori on the eastern shore of the Izu Peninsula. The town was decorated for the festival, with strings of little dolls hanging everywhere. The dolls billowed in the breeze, and their kimono sleeves fluttered gently, waving like silent chimes. This haiku gives me a feeling of peace and rest. My haiku master thought this was a good poem.

I wanted to ask Traveling Man Tree what he meant by "haiku master," but he was now asking me questions. How long had I lived in Japan? Where in America was I from?

I had learned in Japan to rein in my very American habit of revealing a mass of personal details in first encounters. When I did make the mistake of giving long, detailed answers to such questions, the response back was either a nervous giggle or a blank stare. In Japan, my story was simple. *My name is Abigail. I am an American. I grew up in Maryland.* Because my identity is reduced to basics in Japan, I feel more at ease here than anywhere else. In the United States, people look at my frizzy brown hair, glasses, and thin, intense face and say, *Are you sure you're not from New York?* When they learn my mother is from South America, they look at me with skepticism. I try to help them out by saying, *I know I don't look it—I take after my father.* And having a Catholic mother and Jewish father makes me not quite a member of any religious community. In Japan, I am unambiguously, incontrovertibly non-Japanese. I fit the profile perfectly, and so I shed layers of complicated history and am much lighter for it.

Traveling Man Tree next asked if I liked haiku. *Yes, a lot, although I have never written any of my own,* I answered. We were silent for a while. I reread his haiku: *a sea breeze billowing in the sleeve of hanging dolls.* I had never thought of writing my own haiku. Now I wondered why. I found myself answering the question aloud, forgetting my rule of not giving too many personal details in first encounters. *Frankly, I don't think I have a poetic soul! I never kept a journal as a young girl. I never went through that phase of writing poetry as an adolescent. I can't imagine starting to write poetry now.* Traveling Man Tree nodded knowingly and replied, *Oh, lots of Japanese people who never think of themselves as the poetic type write haiku. One of the most famous haiku groups, at the prestigious Tokyo University, has always attracted more science and engineering students than literature majors.*

Neither Traveling Man Tree nor I had been paying much attention to the *aisatsu* ritual, but it was now Traveling Man Tree's turn to offer remarks. He stood up, took the microphone, and motioned to me as he spoke. *I want you to welcome my neighbor. My friend is fond of haiku. She tells me she has never written haiku, but I think perhaps she is just shy. I am sure she writes excellent haiku. Perhaps she will recite some of her work for us tonight.* With that Traveling Man Tree sat down and gave me a wink, and the audience turned to look at me.

What made Traveling Man Tree tell the audience I wrote haiku? I walked up to the microphone, wishing more than ever that I were someplace else. *It's true, I am very fond of Japanese haiku*, I told the small gathering in Japanese. *They are so beautiful and peaceful. But I am afraid Mr. Ōiwa is wrong, I have never written any of my own.*

Then, partly to satisfy the audience and partly to avoid having to reveal any more of myself to strangers, I offered to recite some of my favorite Japanese haiku. The group responded enthusiastically, and so, like a schoolchild, with my hands clasped behind my back, I began to recite a few haiku in Japanese that I had memorized from R. H. Blyth's four-volume work on Japanese haiku. Those volumes were the first, and for many years the only, set of books I owned on the subject.

夕晴れや浅黄に並ぶ秋の山
yūbare ya asagi ni narabu aki no yama

in the evening clear
of a pale blue sky, a row of
fall mountains

KOBAYASHI ISSA (1763–1827)

山くれて紅葉の朱をうばいけり
yama kurete momiji no ake o ubaikeri

the mountain darkens
stealing the crimson
from autumn leaves
　　　YOSA BUSON (1716–83)

故郷も今は假寝や渡り鳥
furusato mo ima wa karine ya wataridori

my childhood home also
now but an evening's lodging—
migrating birds
　　　MUKAI KYORAI (1651–1704)

行く我にとゞまる汝に秋二つ
yuku ware ni todomaru nare ni aki futatsu

I who am going,
and you who remain
two autumns
　　　MASAOKA SHIKI (1867–1902)

After each poem, the audience nodded approval
as one or another recognized a famous haiku. *Ah, Shiki,*
sighed one. *That's Buson!* exclaimed another.[1]

A man in his seventies stood up and said, *I was in
the hospital for an operation last year. Kidney trouble.* As he
spoke, he lifted his shirt, pointed to his kidneys, and made
a cutting motion with his hand. We all leaned closer, to

see his scar. *There I was, lying on my side in a hospital bed in nothing but a flimsy white robe, when suddenly this haiku sprang to mind:*

> 腎臓に管うがたるる酷暑かな
> *jinzō ni kuda ugataruru kokusho kana*

> into my kidney
> a tube pierces
> ah, the summer heat!

The group leaned back and laughed. *Can you believe it? I'm in the hospital, in pain, cranking out a haiku! I sent that haiku in to the* Nihon Keizai Shinbun *newspaper, and they selected it and printed it in their Sunday edition's haiku column. Incredible! To think that's what it took for me to get my haiku published.*

As he told his tale I quietly returned to my seat. Traveling Man Tree had made up a plate of food for me from the buffet: a bowl of cold *soba* noodles, a few cucumber rolls, some sushi and smoked salmon. I set the plate on my lap, pulled the chopsticks out of their paper sheath, and began to eat, as happy as if I was greeting an old friend at the end of the day. Traveling Man Tree watched me with a look of amusement on his face. *You did a great job reciting those haiku. Listen, why don't you join the haiku group I belong to?*

I was flattered by his offer, but protested that I really never had written a haiku in my life. My work kept me busy enough. Traveling Man Tree dismissed my objections. *That doesn't matter. You just have to enjoy haiku. You don't need anything more. We meet once every couple of months in Numazu. Our haiku master is terrific. I have your card. I'll send you an invitation.*

It was getting late, and people were saying their goodbyes. Before we left, we stood in a circle to perform the somewhat old-fashioned customary ending to a party. *Yō . . . oh!* Three sets of three rapid claps performed in unison by everyone present, followed by a single clap and then a round of applause. An elderly Japanese friend once remarked to me that young people in Japan do not seem to follow this custom much anymore, but she had added, almost as an afterthought, *Just wait, though. As the young get older, they too will enjoy traditions.*

Outside, the pavement was wet from rain. I hailed a cab and slid into the back seat. On the way home, I chided myself for having stood up and recited haiku that evening. I must have looked ridiculous. Who ever heard of an American diplomat reciting haiku? I could only console myself with the thought that I would never see any of these people again.

two

CASCADING CRIES OF THE CICADA

Traveling Man Tree's invitation arrived in the mail about a month later. The Numamomo haiku group, it read, would next meet at the Goyōtei, in the town of Numazu, on Saturday, October 5, from one to five in the afternoon. I had no idea what Numamomo or Goyōtei meant, and no one I asked at my office had ever been to Numazu. One of my colleagues, a native of Tokyo, said with a tone of disdain, *It must be one of those small towns in the countryside somewhere.* After some searching, I found the town on the map. It looked to be about an hour and a half west of Tokyo by train, in the vicinity of Mount Fuji.

That Saturday, leaving my family behind, I took the bullet train out of Tokyo to Mishima, the transfer point to popular tourist destinations south on the Izu Peninsula. It was the first time since having children that I was taking a trip unrelated to work, alone. I traveled so much for my job that it was hard for me to leave my family simply for pleasure. But the train sped along and I began to relax, catching glimpses from my window of the surface of the bay glimmering in the sun, stretching out toward the horizon. An apartment building whizzed into sight, blocking my view of the sea. Moments later it was gone, and the sea and curve of the horizon reappeared. Another building appeared, blocked the sea, became a blur, and vanished in a blink.

How strange life is! Fifteen years ago, I was sitting in a bed at Dr. Takahara's Lady Clinic holding my newborn son, wondering how I had ended up in Hiroshima and what it all meant. I was far from home and did not know the first thing about babies. I pored over child-rearing manuals as if they were science textbooks, trying to figure out why my baby was crying. I had spent four years in college studying the history of science and another three years studying law, and now I was supposed to intuitively know how to handle a baby.

One evening, my husband came home and, as he watched me struggling to breastfeed our son, sighed, *I don't think this housewife role is right for you. You really should follow up with the Foreign Service.* I had passed the Foreign Service exam before leaving the United States but had been lackadaisical in pursuing the option. I was having a hard time picturing myself as a diplomat. I recalled the scene well: our colicky baby had bit me, squirmed, and started to cry. *Well, maybe you are right,* I said, handing him the baby. A few months later we booked train tickets to Tokyo, so that I could complete my application there. Soon after that, I entered the Foreign Service.

I thought that once I joined the Foreign Service we would come back to Japan. Instead we were sent to the Azores, windswept islands in the middle of the Atlantic. After that our life became a series of checkerboard moves, with assignments in Washington, Tokyo, Washington, Paris, and again Tokyo. Fifteen years, seven moves, and two more children later, I was back in Japan sitting on a train, this time heading out of Tokyo, past beautiful scenery, toward a town and people I did not know. I was midway through my second Japan assignment and no more certain of where I fit in the world as the day when, cradling my crying baby in Hiroshima, I first decided to join the Foreign Service. I had a great job, three energetic children, and a husband I loved dearly. So why was I still in a restless search? What was I looking for? The sea disappeared and appeared and disappeared again.

I was one of only a handful of passengers who changed trains at Mishima that day for the local to Numazu, in the foothills of Mount Fuji, far from the peninsula's luxurious beaches and mountain retreats. We rattled past cement-block buildings, laundry lines, and electric wires, arriving at a forlorn station with two bare platforms and no roof overhead. I had expected clean, crisp views of Mount Fuji from the train. Instead, the only image of the mountain I saw was in the station when I got off the train, splashed on posters advertising everything from English-language institutes to cut-rate business hotels. Outside, too, images of Fuji adorned the stands near the station that sold dried fish snacks and bean-paste-filled sweets. In Numazu, Japan's most famous mountain was reduced to a marketing device.

In front of the station, I found and got on the bus for Goyōtei, that still-mysterious destination. Like the train, the bus was almost empty. A thin old man in worn, shiny pants sat close to the driver at the front. A little further back, another elderly man in a faded fedora and a once-fine suit sat patiently waiting for the bus to start. A desultory young woman in a soft red leather Italian jacket and a knee-length black wool skirt stepped onto the bus. She looked around, found a seat far from all of us, and marked her territory by placing a large leather bag on the empty seat beside her.

I tried to guess which of my fellow passengers might be going to the Goyōtei for a haiku session. Other than my brief acquaintance with Traveling Man Tree, I had no sense of what a contemporary Japanese haiku writer might look like. The only other person I knew who wrote haiku was a French woman I had met five years earlier, when I was posted to Paris. Until then, "haiku" was just one more poetic term, like "sonnet" or "iambic pentameter," tucked away in a drawer in my mind marked "poetry," ready for me to pull out in the event that a conversation ever turned to that subject. But my friend from France, Elizabeth Guinsbourg, wrote haiku. She showed me a journal she kept in her purse, where she jotted down haiku as they came to mind. Writing haiku for her was a spontaneous, uncomplicated act.

pluie bienvenue si
je ne songe pas à regretter
le soleil d'hier
rain welcome if
I don't think to regret
yesterday's sunshine

métro: un type porte
une vieille selle de vélo dans
une cage à oiseaux
subway: some guy is
carrying an old bike saddle
inside a birdcage

dans une vitrine en
passant j'ai vu le visage
de la fille qui t'aime
in a window in
passing I saw the face of
the girl who loves you

ELIZABETH GUINSBOURG
(both French and English)

Elizabeth had already published one book of haiku
and by the time I left France she was well underway on her
second. She was a strikingly handsome woman with black
eyes glowing with artistic passion. If anyone on the bus
was a haiku writer, I was sure it must be the classy woman
in the red leather jacket.

The light changed and the bus lurched forward. Numazu was unremarkable in every way. We passed coffee shops with ersatz French names, a shop selling plastic buckets, a string of fast-food restaurants, and a row of car dealers. I began to regret wasting my first holiday without my family on this town.

From somewhere above my head the silken, recorded voice of a woman purred the name of each stop. When I was growing up in the America of the 1960s, the recorded voice of machines or movie documentaries was always optimistic, matter-of-fact, confident, and male. Sometime in the 1980s, the voice became assertive, instructive, and female. The voice of early postwar Japan, which I knew from documentaries, had been bright, sunny, and male. Today, on this bus, as everywhere in Japan, the recorded voice was young, cute, and female. Change was happening in Japan, but I was unsure in which direction it was heading.

Numazu's commercial strip eventually gave way to private homes packed close together. The bus rounded a corner and pulled to a stop. The recorded voice announced, *Goyōtei, Goyōtei. Please watch your step. Please don't forget your belongings.* The woman in the red leather jacket buffed her fingernails and made no move to get off the bus. The gentleman in the fedora, however, had stepped off the bus and was walking briskly toward a high iron gate. I got up, paid my fare, and followed after him.

A wooden sign near the iron gate marked it as the Goyōtei. I stepped through the gate and found myself in a richly wooded stretch of land, wrapped in quiet. I stood silent, breathing in the scent of pine mixed with the salt air of the sea. I closed my eyes. I was far, far from Tokyo.

I had lost track of the man in the fedora, but a gatekeeper in a wooden hut handed me a brochure with a map of the area and a description of the Goyōtei. I now learned it was once a summer retreat for the imperial family. Like many imperial holdings the Goyōtei had been turned over to public use after the war. I asked the gatekeeper if a haiku session was being held on the grounds. Unaccustomed to hearing a foreigner speak Japanese, he used hand motions, pointing first to a low, Japanese-style wooden building at the far end of the grounds, and then to the impeccably clean slate walkway I was to take to get there.

I walked up to the low building, toward a gathering of about thirty elderly-looking men and women who were taking off their shoes and placing them in cubbyholes at the entryway. Everyone bowed and smiled at me as I neared, and I bowed and smiled back. I was the only non-Japanese in the group, and my longtime habit of setting myself apart from others kicked in.

I had never been to a haiku group, and was not much for joining groups in general. A feeling of paranoia grew within me. What if this turned out to be a cult? An American colleague in Japan once told me of being invited by strangers into their home. After taking off his shoes and entering the house, he realized the strangers were members of a pseudoreligious cult. They smiled and offered him tea and talked to him of spiritual salvation, but would not let him leave. Hours later, after much negotiation and growing panic on his part, his hosts relented and gave him back his shoes. I placed my shoes in the cubbyhole with some anxiety, but resisted the urge to carry them in with me.

Then again, the group might just as easily be a hotbed of Japanese far-right nationalism. After all, haiku had a long historical tradition in Japan, and we were meeting on grounds once owned by the imperial household. Or the haiku group might be a far-left association. My years as a diplomat analyzing political trends were distorting my judgment. Still, I made a mental note to check whether McCarthy-era laws remained in place, and whether I might be fired for membership in a Communist Party haiku group.

Whatever the nature of the group, there was no turning back. We were all making our way now down a narrow hallway. We turned right into a very large room, about twenty by thirty feet, with a high cedar ceiling and a tatami-mat floor where we were to sit Japanese-style. A delicately carved sheet of thin cedar spanned the ceiling at its midpoint, providing the room's only decorative touch. Sliding paper screen doors along one wall hid recessed closets. Facing me, another set of sliding doors opened onto a glass-walled, enclosed wooden balcony that ran the length of the building. The room, rich with the scent of cedar and tatami, was beautiful in its simplicity.

A Japanese garden beckoned beyond the balcony, through windowpanes wavy with age. Toward the back of the garden, near a bamboo fence, stood an old stone lantern, squat and mossy—the kind that I had until then seen only in old prints of Japan. It was a "snow viewing," or *yuki-mi,* lantern, so named because it is most beautiful when capped with snow. I could hardly believe that I was a part of this exquisite scene. Its sheer beauty calmed my fears.

Several members of the haiku group were taking low, folding tables out of the recessed closets and arranging them in a large rectangle around the room. Others sat on the tatami, placing their pens and rice-paper notebooks on the low tables. I spotted Traveling Man Tree seated in the far corner. Next to him was the man with the fedora who had been on the bus. He and Traveling Man Tree were absorbed in conversation with a third man, who was quite distinguished-looking in his three-piece suit. I hesitated, wondering where to sit, when two women smiled at me and patted the tatami between them. Relieved that I was no longer isolated, I went over to them, stepping over people to get there, bowing and excusing myself on the way.

The two women told me they were from Kamakura, the medieval capital of Japan, about an hour south of Tokyo by train. They had come up together for the haiku session. The first woman, graceful and of slender build, spoke to me in excellent English. She said she was a historian and her haiku name was Chōon, or "Sound of the Tide." She had lived in the United States for six and a half years, she explained, having followed her husband there when the Japanese bank he worked for transferred him to New York.

Sound of the Tide introduced me to her friend,

whose haiku name was Uono, or Fish Field. Fish Field, brimming with energy, gave me a big smile. She appeared to be one of the younger members of the group, perhaps in her late forties. Fish Field told me she was a caricature artist, a Japanese word I did not understand until she took out one of her calling cards to show me. The card had a self-portrait in the upper right corner—a caricature with a peppy smile, jet-black hair, and bright, intelligent eyes behind huge, round glasses. Fish Field made room for me at the table. How could someone so likeable have such a strange haiku name? Fish Field evoked a field of smelly, rotting fish. In my mind I called her "Field and Stream," after the fishing magazine—a name that I found just as humorous but that evoked a more pleasant image.

I turned my attention back to Sound of the Tide. She intrigued me. I had always thought of haiku as an art focused on the present moment, where words came from a flash of poetic inspiration or were triggered by a scene, a sound, or even a scent. Yet here was Sound of the Tide, a historian devoted to researching the past, taking up the art. I could not understand why she would be attracted to haiku. I asked and she replied, *I love doing historical research. But history is like doing a jigsaw puzzle. It is solitary and demands patience. I was looking for an activity that would involve more people. I was searching for something, but I did not know quite what.*

I had never thought of haiku, or any kind of poetry for that matter, as a social activity. I assumed people wrote haiku to connect with themselves, in keeping with my image of the Zen monk writing haiku in the woods. Yet here was Sound of the Tide telling me that she was attracted to haiku because it would connect her with others.

Sound of the Tide explained that at about the time she was looking for something to add to her life, she learned that Field and Stream was starting up a haiku group in Kamakura. She had never written haiku at that point, but she joined Field and Stream's group. Some months later, when they learned that Dr. Mochizuki was forming a group in Numazu, she and Field and Stream joined that group too. Hearing mention of Dr. Mochizuki, Field and Stream pointed out to me the elderly gentleman I had noticed earlier sitting with Traveling Man Tree and the man with the fedora. *That's him. He's the organizer of our group. He's a doctor and an essayist.*

I asked Field and Stream why she joined the Numamomo haiku group. *Me? I joined because Kuroda Momoko is the haiku master. I've read some of her books and I like her openness of spirit. Also, I thought it would be great to do haiku in a place as beautiful as the Goyōtei!*

I was nodding in agreement when the sliding paper screen door opened behind us. The room became quiet and I turned to see an exotic woman in her sixties walk in. I knew instantly that this must be the person Traveling Man Tree and Field and Stream referred to as our haiku master. Her salt-and-pepper hair was cropped like a schoolgirl's—bangs straight across her forehead and then falling in an even cut about an inch above her shoulders, framing a deeply wrinkled, peaceful face. She smiled at us as she entered, and more deep creases broke forth around her eyes. She wore an unusual outfit, which appeared to be a modern variation on the traditional Japanese *samue*—a cotton wraparound blouse with loose, matching, calf-length pants. Our haiku master's version of the *samue* was deep indigo, with white stitching in traditional Japanese geometric patterns. I have never seen anyone in Japan dress like her, before or since.

Our haiku master settled herself in at one of the low tables and gave us all a reassuring nod and bow. Traveling Man Tree leaned over to Momoko and mentioned that several of us were new to the group. She spoke:

It's good to see so many new faces this month. If this is your first time, do not worry, I am sure you will do just fine. The most important thing for you today is not to think about whether your haiku is "good enough."

Don't try to write a haiku that is "like Bashō's" or "like Issa's."

Work on developing a haiku that truly reflects you. If you can write a haiku that expresses you, then you are writing a good haiku.

My job is not to judge whether you have written well or poorly, but to help you write a haiku that is true to yourself.

We can each write haiku because we each have a soul. Every soul is equal in a haiku group, and there is room in a haiku group for every soul.

By listening to the haiku of others, you will learn about yourself and your haiku. And others in turn will learn about themselves through your haiku.

With that, the session began. Someone handed me five long, narrow strips of paper and told me to write down five haiku. I desperately tried to create haiku on the spot but could not even decide which language to write in, much less a theme. I turned to Sound of the Tide, who had just finished writing out:

蝉しぐれ句を練る人等美しく
semishigure ku o neru hitora utsukushiku

the beauty of
people struggling with haiku
cascading cries of the cicada
SOUND OF THE TIDE

Did that haiku come to you right now? I mean, are you receiving some inspiration? I asked. *Of course not*, she answered. *I am only writing down the best five I've written over the past two months.*

I looked around the room. Silence reigned. People knelt on the floor and bent low over their work, copying out their haiku. I stared at my five blank strips of paper. *Now I am really in over my head*, I thought. Here was a serious group of poets and I had just come here to . . . well, why had I come here? As an adventure? On a lark? I looked down at my strips of paper, which were as blank as my mind.

Slowly, words began to percolate inside me, and I jotted them down. As soon as I had a string of seventeen syllables, I moved on to the next. In all, I wrote down five haiku that first day: three in English and two in Japanese. They were not even mildly good haiku. Haiku should be spontaneous and come from within, I had read. These were desperate and pulled out of thin air. But that day, they were all I had.

Someone passed an empty cardboard box around the room, and we all put our five strips of paper in the box facedown. As poor as my haiku were, at least they were now out of my hands. I leaned over to Field and Stream and asked her again the name of our teacher.

She whispered back, *Kuroda Momoko, but she's just Momoko-sensei to us. She is very active. She's written many books on haiku and won prizes for her works. She has a column every Sunday in the* Nikkei *newspaper, and she often appears on haiku programs on television. But don't let any of that intimidate you. She is very thoughtful and will be very respectful of your work.*

The cardboard box came around again, and this time we each pulled five haiku strips from the box at random. Sound of the Tide, sitting next to me, told me to copy these five haiku onto a single sheet of paper. When everyone finished this task, we passed the sheets around the room. There were a total of about thirty sheets, one for each member of the group, including Momoko. As the sheets came around one by one, we read the haiku, and if a particular haiku struck our fancy, we wrote it down on a sheet of paper. At the end of the session, after reading about 150 haiku, we were to narrow our selection down to our five favorites and read these aloud to the group.

Sound of the Tide must have seen the look of confusion on my face. She turned to me and explained: *The idea is to ensure anonymity. We write our haiku down on strips of paper without our names on them. But if we choose our favorite haiku just from the strips of paper, we might still be able to guess from the handwriting whose they are. On the single sheet, they are in someone else's handwriting, so it is really hard to guess who wrote them.* I had watched Momoko write down her five haiku on strips of paper and put them in the cardboard box with the rest of us. It would be easy to feel obliged to choose Momoko's haiku, or to pay homage to Dr. Mochizuki, our group's organizer, by picking his haiku. Equality and artistic integrity, I was learning, are essential aspects of a haiku group.

After reading through the sheets of haiku and choosing our favorites, but before reading them aloud, we took a break. I was one of the last still reading and writing. My legs were numb from kneeling Japanese-style at the low table. A woman came up to me and said, *It hurts to sit like that, doesn't it? There's really no need to do so for such a long period of time.* I looked around the room and saw that most of the men had been sitting cross-legged and many women had shifted from a straight kneeling position to tucking their legs slightly to the side. One woman had her legs straight out on the tatami and was wiggling her toes as she chatted with her neighbor. *Here, try this,* said the woman as she folded a *zabuton* pillow over and pushed it beneath my legs. I had been trying hard, too hard, to be Japanese.

When everyone was done and our short break ended, we moved on to the next phase of the session. Beginning with the person to the right of Momoko, we each read aloud the five anonymous haiku we had selected. After each reading, the author of the haiku announced himself or herself to the group.

My turn came and I read out the following haiku:

被爆後の生命をつなぐぶどう棚
hibakugo no inochi o tsunagu budōdana

after the bombing
life hangs on
to the grapevine trellis
TRAVELING MAN TREE

あかつきの夏富士の上星ひとつ
akatsuki no natsufuji no ue hoshi hitotsu

summer dawn
above Mount Fuji
a single star
SOUND OF THE POND

本を措くやがて秋富士見ゆる頃
hon o oku yagate akifuji miyuru koro

I set aside my book
Mount Fuji soon appears
in autumn form
DANCE

風の香ににじむ水色手漉き和紙
kaze no ka ni nijimu mizuiro tesuki washi

the scent of a breeze
wafts pale blue
washi paper
FIELD AND STREAM

掛物を水墨にかへ夕涼み
kakemono o suiboku ni kae yūsuzumi

black ink hanging scroll
now changed
the evening breeze blows cool
OKA TAKEHIDE

Momoko was the last person to read out haiku. Instead of limiting herself to five haiku, Momoko read, commented on, and praised about forty of them. She would take a haiku and use it to illustrate a point or offer a suggestion, peppering her commentary with stories about her own life and writing:

As a child, I learned how to write haiku at my mother's side. It wasn't until I went to college that I joined a haiku group. There was a famous haiku poet at my college, Yamaguchi Seison. My mother told me I should write to him and tell him of my interest in haiku. I did so because of my mother's encouragement, and that's how I joined a haiku group.

Sometimes, while reading aloud, she would stop and give us insights into the shared enjoyment of haiku.

It is wonderful to write haiku alone, to contemplate it, to read and reread it, and to polish it in private. We can learn a lot about our writing doing this. Yet joining with others and sharing haiku is an essential part of the haiku experience. Think about what a haiku represents. This small chalice of only seventeen sounds is, in truth, an expression of the nature of your heart and soul. There is something magical about sharing this piece of yourself with friends who have gathered together to read haiku aloud.

The Numamomo haiku group was filled with a spirit of warmth and common purpose. We were doing haiku as a group, but instead of social pressure I felt as in a warm embrace. Kuroda Momoko did not tell us what is beautiful, but asked us to judge beauty on our own terms. This was unlike learning experiences I had had at school or at work, and there was no place for my competitive streak. The only expectation seemed to be that I contribute haiku true to myself. I left Numazu brimming with enthusiasm, determined to come up with at least one good, "true-to-myself" haiku for our next gathering. Of course, I had no idea how to do this.

three

DUCKS IN THE PALACE MOAT

By the end of the week, I knew I needed remedial help. Like a self-taught swimmer who knows nothing about breathing or stroke technique, I was having trouble figuring out the basics of writing haiku.

I also was having trouble making the time for my haiku. Before joining the Foreign Service, I held a wonderfully romantic view of the life of a diplomat, the product of my fertile imagination and of watching too many old movies. To me, the word "diplomat" evoked a Katharine Hepburn–esque figure in a long trench coat, somewhere in London at night, knocking desperately on Winston Churchill's door. She breaks into a state dinner party and passes a message to the great man just in time to stop the German forces from advancing further into Europe. Or in Italy, against a backdrop of blue sky and glittering ocean, a diplomat in a red sports car deftly takes the curves of the Amalfi drive, throwing her head back in laughter at a remark made by the handsome young Italian beside her.

My life as a diplomat was a far cry from these images. In Tokyo I had the North Korea portfolio, and North Korea was the problem child of Asia. The country was a totalitarian dictatorship that was developing nuclear weapons and had missiles pointed at Japan. North Korea tolerated no dissent, ran huge gulags, and kept its economy afloat through counterfeit currency and the drug trade. As if all of this was not enough, North Korea had recently admitted to kidnapping Japanese citizens, including a young girl whisked off the beach while on her way home from badminton practice back in 1973. I was spending my days in office buildings and coffee shops, talking to people, wanting to understand how Japan was reacting to events in North Korea, and writing up what I learned in a way that I hoped made sense to Washington. Japan was our ally. We needed to understand the mood and thinking in Japan, just as the Japanese needed to understand our thinking.

I did not want to talk only to government officials. I wanted to know what the average Japanese person felt when North Korea reminded the world, ominously, that Japan was within "striking distance." Did the average person give thought to the question of in what circumstances Japan should defend itself? Was the standoff with North Korea a real and immediate worry, or something more removed? What did people think about the kidnappings? Were they angry at North Korea, their own government, or both?

When North Korea admitted to kidnapping Japanese citizens, the focus in Japan seemed to shift from North

Korea's nuclear and missile programs to the human dimension. This was a preoccupation for me too. When I left the office, I would walk home in the dark thinking not about haiku but about Yokota Megumi, the young girl who had been kidnapped many years earlier. My daughter was thirteen, the same age Megumi had been when she was abducted by North Korean spies. I would get home, go into my daughter's room, and kiss her as she slept, wondering how I would ever cope if one day she just never came home.

I was working long hours helping to keep Washington up-to-date. Much of my work in Tokyo was like that of a reporter, and because Tokyo is thirteen hours ahead of the U.S. capital, I would set myself a late evening deadline, so that Washington would have the latest information when it woke up in the morning.

At work, my boss was urging us all to pace ourselves and to get some rest. The North Korea situation would not be resolved quickly. I decided to renew my commitment to haiku, despite the hectic pace at work. Late one evening I sat down at the dining room table and wrote a letter in polite Japanese to my haiku master.

> *Dear Honorable Kuroda Momoko,*
> *It is the season of the fragrance of chrysanthemums. I*
> *trust that you are doing well. Thank you for all of your*
> *kind help at the Numamomo haiku group.*
>
> *Forgive me for jumping into this request right*
> *away, but might it be possible for you to provide me*

with additional help in learning haiku? If you agree, I could meet you at a time and place convenient to you.

Please accept my apology for burdening you with this request. Please continue to favor me with your guidance. I wish you good health.

Momoko wrote back a week later on thick, handcrafted rice paper. *Our hearts are similar, perhaps we were born under the same star.* She wrote that she would be pleased to help. There was no need for me to pay her, as we would both gain from the experience. I took a day off from work to prepare for my first haiku session with Momoko.

I had read that Bashō, the seventeenth-century father of Japanese haiku, wrote some of his best haiku while wandering through the natural beauty of rural Japan. I did not have time for a long trip but hoped to capture the haiku spirit with a walk through the grounds of the imperial palace, Tokyo's equivalent of Manhattan's Central Park. Once owned by the shoguns, the grounds passed to the Meiji Emperor in the mid-nineteenth century and remain an imperial family holding to this day. Although much of the grounds are off limits, there are still miles of walking paths open to the public.

I waited that morning until my husband and children were out the door, then filled a thermos with coffee, threw on my pea jacket, grabbed my electronic English-Japanese pocket dictionary, and headed to the park, about a twenty-minute walk from my home along a busy thoroughfare.

It was morning rush hour in Tokyo. Oddly, this is a

pleasant time for pedestrians: there are so many cars on the road that all of them are at a complete standstill. I jaywalked across the street, debating with myself. What was more urgent, North Korea's human rights violations or its nuclear weapons programs? Several people fleeing North Korea had told of concentration-camp-like holding areas for political and other prisoners; large swaths of the population had nothing to eat; and the North Korean government itself had admitted to kidnapping Japanese citizens. At the same time, we were grappling with North Korea's nuclear weapons programs.

What was the correct relationship between the strategic and the individual in foreign affairs? President Roosevelt had chosen not to bomb the concentration camps or the train tracks leading to them early in World War II, because these were not "strategic priorities." The world failed to intercede and stop the slaughter in Rwanda because saving innocent souls did not rise to the level of a strategic imperative. Couldn't we have stopped Milosevic's destructive designs in the Balkans earlier? What about human rights violations in North Korea? Didn't history teach us that the dismissal of these violations triggered dramatic consequences that were in themselves "strategic"? It was impossible to work on North Korea and not think about such moral dilemmas. I worried about the collective responsibility and guilt we would bear when the truth of North Korea's horrible treatment of its own people became more widely known.

The road came to an end sooner than I expected, and

I found myself standing before the imperial palace moat. Across the moat, a steep grassy hill led up to the old castle rampart. I imagined warriors of ancient times entering the gates, pulling their horses to a sharp halt in a cloud of dust, bringing reports of peasant rebellions and battles won or lost. Courtesans would have walked upon these same grounds, composing poetry while gazing on this same moat.

I was unsure whether history was an acceptable haiku topic, then remembered this one by Bashō:

夏草やつわものどもが夢のあと
natsukusa ya tsuwamono domo ga yume no ato

summer grasses—
all that remains
of warriors' dreams[2]
MATSUO BASHŌ (1644–94)

Bashō had written this haiku while looking out over the fields of Takadachi in northern Japan, where a legendary twelfth-century battle took place. His poem reminded me of one I learned in high school, *Ozymandias* by Percy Bysshe Shelley:

... And on the pedestal these words appear:
"My name is Ozymandias, king of kings:
Look on my works, ye Mighty, and despair!"

Nothing beside remains. Round the decay
of that colossal wreck, boundless and bare
The lone and level sands stretch far away.

A duck paddled about in the black, uninviting waters
of the moat. The wind was picking up. I turned up my collar and dug my hands deeper into my pockets. I stopped
thinking of North Korea or history or battles and found
myself more and more interested in the duck. He seemed
uncertain of his direction, as if he too was feeling the cold.
Despite the darkness of the water, I could just make out
his webbed feet moving rapidly beneath the surface.

A haiku took shape within me:

秋の風皇居の濠の鴨の足
aki no kaze kōkyo no hori no kamo no ashi

the fall wind
in the palace moat
a duck's feet

I knew this was not a good haiku. "A duck's feet"
sounded silly in English. It probably sounded just as bad
in Japanese. The haiku did not capture the scene or my
mood. Sighing, I wrote it down on a scrap of paper, tucked
it in my pocket, and returned home. I couldn't wait for my
first meeting with Momoko.

❀　❀　❀

Momoko arrived at my home on a Saturday afternoon, wrapped in a black wool cape. She had a natural ease about her, the self-confidence born of self-acceptance that is the true beauty of women as they age. My family had gone to the movies, and our apartment was hollow and quiet. Momoko filled the space with her presence. She wore the same kind of *samue*-like tunic under her cape as she had when I first met her in Numazu. It was her first time visiting my inordinately spacious American-style apartment, but she barely took notice of the room.

I had read up on Momoko since meeting her in Numazu. She was born in 1938, on the eve of World War II. While most women of her generation settled into the traditional role of homemaker, Momoko went her own way. Even after marrying she continued working, first for an advertising agency and later as a haiku poet. She marched against the Vietnam War and opposed the war in Iraq, yet she took pride in the range of political views held by her haiku followers. She was the embodiment of independent thought and action, and respected independence in others as well.

Everyone is capable of writing haiku, writes Momoko in one of her books on haiku for beginners. Momoko traveled the countryside, meeting would-be haiku poets. Our haiku group in Numazu was only one of many such seminars that she led around the country. She often appeared on television, and for a while she also had her own web page where she posted a new haiku of her own each day. In 1990, after the death of her haiku mentor Yamaguchi

Seison, Momoko founded and became editor-in-chief of a subscriber-funded haiku journal, *Aoi*. All *Aoi* subscribers, from beginner to advanced, could send their haiku to the journal and see their work in print. Momoko believed in haiku for the people.

Let's see what you have written. Momoko walked over toward my large dining room table as she spoke, taking off her cape and settling into a chair as naturally as if she were my aunt.

I hesitated, picking at scraps of paper where I had scribbled down a few haiku in a mixture of wobbly Japanese characters and romanized script. At last, I pulled out my "duck's feet" haiku and showed it to her.

So, she began, leaning forward, *tell me about this haiku. Where were you when you thought of it? What were you feeling?* As I described the scene, my mood, and what I was trying to express, Momoko pulled toward her a pad of lined paper that had been lying on the table. She spoke, writing down terms in Japanese as she went along:

We need to begin by going over the elements of haiku. A haiku is composed of three basic elements: seasonal words, seventeen sounds, and kireji, *or "cut-words." Today let's concentrate on seasonal words.*

When you read a haiku or are writing your own, you need to think of language in a different way. A haiku is only seventeen sounds, so each word has to count. Momoko explained that some words, in addition to describing an object or event, are also associated with a season. For example, a dandelion is associated with spring. Falling leaves are associated with winter. *We call these* kigo, *or seasonal words. Think of* kigo *as the power-packed, subatomic particles hidden in your haiku.* Kigo *give extra thrust to your poem because they both represent an object or event and evoke an entire seasonal setting.*

Momoko pointed to the word "duck" in my haiku. *To a haiku writer, "duck" is a winter* kigo. *But in your haiku, you include the phrase "fall wind." You are mixing seasonal images and confusing the reader. Your haiku lacks harmony.*

As odd, I suppose, as writing about sunflowers in the snow. Momoko told me that I could make "duck" symbolize different seasons through qualifiers: *"Ducks crossing," for example, evokes ducks in the fall migrating south for the winter, making it an autumn* kigo.

Momoko turned her pad of paper sideways, so that the blue lines printed on the sheets fell vertically. She wrote the old-fashioned Japanese way, from top to bottom and starting at the top right-hand corner of the page:

鴨来る
kamo kitaru
ducks arriving

You can identify the season simply by using the fall kigo *"ducks arriving."* I pictured ducks arriving at the palace moat to rest briefly before heading south. *By using this term, you do not need to refer to the fall directly. You have referred to the image of ducks and captured the season, with just that one phrase.*

I looked at my work again. Until now, I had not given seasonal words much thought. I considered them a technicality and did not see how they could help me write good haiku.

In English too, I realized, qualifying a word could alter its seasonal context—ice versus ice melting; birds versus birds flying south or birds molting. *Some words in English also have a seasonal connotation*, I said. *Perhaps a turkey would be a fall seasonal word in English because of its association with Thanksgiving.*

So, so, so, she replied, using the friendly idiom of everyday Japanese speech. We sat peacefully at the dining room table, the afternoon light skimming the surface of the table. Like soft music filling the living room, Momoko spoke of the fluidity of language, the seasons, and haiku.

Our seasonal words have been collected over the years in what we call a saijiki, *a kind of index of seasonal words. The concept of a* saijiki *originated in China over a thousand years ago. At first Japanese scholars and poets worked from Chinese* saijiki, *but over time we developed our own, with words that arose from Japanese culture and tradition.*

Momoko pointed out that some words, like "snow," are obvious seasonal words, but that others are harder to place. A *saijiki* works as a seasonal word reference manual, containing several thousand such words and phrases, from "baby sparrow" to "falling leaves" and "knitted scarf."

I asked Momoko who decides which words make it into a *saijiki*. Is there a Japanese equivalent of the Academie Française that rules on the proper use of French terms? Momoko seemed puzzled by the question and then assured me that there is no formal process or academy to decide which words are *kigo*. A consensus simply emerges among haiku masters.

Momoko suggested that owning a *saijiki*, or seasonal dictionary, would help me figure out which words were *kigo*. She showed me a pocket seasonal dictionary she carried in her purse, and we turned the pages until we found the listing for duck:

kamo (duck). Also, mallard. Winter seasonal word.

And under that heading:

Spring seasonal words: Ducks returning; returning ducks; remaining ducks; spring duck; ducks heading out; ducks passing . . .
Summer seasonal words: Ducklings; ducks parting; summer ducks; losing-their-feathers ducks . . .
Fall seasonal words: Ducks arriving; ducks crossing; first ducks . . .
Winter seasonal words: Ducks calling; the voice of the ducks; duck pond; duck soup . . .[3]

Following this came several illustrative haiku:

海暮れて鴨の声ほのかに白し
umi kurete kamo no koe honoka ni shiroshi

sea at dusk
the call of a duck
a faint white
BASHŌ

着水の鴨もしぶきも前のめり
chakusui no kamo mo shibuki mo mae nomeri

landing in the water
a duck and a splash
both pitching forward
TEZUKA MISA (1934–)

In flipping through her pocket seasonal dictionary, I noticed that some animals were listed, but others were not. Frog was listed as a spring seasonal word, and rabbit as a winter seasonal word. But rat was not listed. I asked Momoko what I should do if a word is not in the *saijiki*.

Well, of course you can still write a haiku about an animal that is not listed—just use another word in the haiku as the seasonal word, she answered. I recalled this one, by Buson:

皿を踏む鼠の音の寒さかな
Sara o fumu nezumi no oto no samusa kana

cold as the sound of a rat on a plate
BUSON

And what if you are in Hokkaido in the middle of a

snowstorm, but the season is actually fall? I asked. Momoko seemed not bothered in the least by all my questions.

Your question makes sense. There are regional varia-tions. For example, cherry blossom is a spring seasonal word but in Okinawa to the south, cherry trees bloom before spring. In Hokkaido to the north, cherry trees might not bloom until June or July!

Momoko explained that during the Edo period, from the mid-seventeenth through the mid-nineteenth cen-turies, *saijiki* were based on the seasons, foods, and cus-toms of Kyoto. Later *saijiki* began to reflect the seasons as they appear in Tokyo. Momoko told me there was a movement underway to decentralize and create regional and local *saijiki*, precisely because of the problem I had pointed out.

There are other challenges in deciding what season a word might fall under, she continued. *A tomato is a summer* kigo, *but nowadays tomatoes are grown in greenhouses or flown in from other parts of the world year round. Should a tomato re-main a summer seasonal word? Should it be dropped from the* saijiki? Momoko said the consensus among haiku poets was that the summer tomato tastes best and is the arche-type, so it has been retained as a summer kigo.

Sensing perhaps that I was still not altogether buying into the idea of seasonal words, Momoko tried a different approach.

Do you know the true power of a seasonal word? These words do not belong to the author of the poem, they do not belong to Bashō or Issa or Kyorai. They belong to us. Seasonal words are our national treasures. They are like jewels, polished and made more precious by time. Some seasonal words have been in use since the Edo period. When we pick up one of these jewels and use it in a haiku, it is rich with history. They are the shared consciousness of our people. They capture the essence of Japanese life.

Momoko was bringing it back to national identity and history. She took the pad of paper and wrote:

霧時雨 富士を見ぬ ひぞ 面白き
kirishigure fuji o minu hi zo omoshiroki

a misty shower
I can't see Mount Fuji
delightful days!
BASHŌ

Bashō uses the term kirishigure, *or misty shower, as five sounds of his seventeen-sound haiku. Even so, this term is not considered his alone. We are all welcome to use this phrase. When you write a poem using the seasonal word "misty shower," you are connecting yourself back hundreds of years to the era of Bashō. His spirit comes alive again in your haiku. Seasonal words unify people, not only in the present but also with the past.*

I got up to make us some coffee. What Momoko was teaching me about seasonal words made sense in Japanese, but I was less sure the idea made sense in English. There is no rich history, no linkage with the poetic past for a seasonal word to evoke in English. Would "ducks arriving" have the same impact and dual meaning (as both an image and a seasonal word) as in Japanese? I did not see how this would make my haiku resonate with beauty. On the other hand, understanding that a word can represent both an object and a season did make sense for me in English. I did not have to use the word "winter" in a haiku if I was already using the word "snow."

I served Momoko coffee and sat down. She picked up where we left off:

Of the thousands of seasonal words you might find in a large saijiki, *perhaps five hundred can be considered fundamental. If you become familiar with these five hundred, you will have great knowledge not simply of Japanese haiku, but of Japanese life, culture, and traditions.*

But please remember that not everyone writing haiku in Japan believes in seasonal words or considers them essential to haiku. I am teaching you what is important to me. I believe that seasonal words are a valuable, attractive part of haiku.

Outside, an ambulance, horn wailing, pushed its way through traffic backed up on the expressway, and we waited for the noise to pass. Momoko and I were talking about the beauty of seasonal words in one of most densely populated cities in the world. Millions of Tokyoites live in apartments surrounded by a jungle of highways and high-rises. Nature, flowers, the seasons—all are far removed from the daily life of many Japanese. I began to feel that Momoko's respect for seasonal words was an aspect of her humanism. For Momoko, rooting haiku in nature was a way of nurturing a humanity too easily eroded by modern life.

My husband and children had come back from the movies some time ago and quietly gone into another room. I had announced that morning that my haiku master would be coming over. Now, as early evening crept up, all three children neared the dining room, circling silently like hungry bears. I knew they were curious, but they did not interrupt us. They were deeply respectful in her presence.

Momoko sensed it was getting late, and she stood up to put on her cape. My children moved back, with their eyes glued to her. Momoko smiled at them and walked past them with a twinkle in her eye. She understood that children sometimes need to observe, without necessarily needing to engage in conversation. As she reached the door she stopped, with her hand on the doorknob, as if she had just remembered something. She walked back to the table, studied my duck haiku, picked up a pen, and wrote:

鴨来る皇居の濠にわれもまた
kamo kitaru kōkyo no hori ni ware mo mata

ducks arriving
at the imperial palace moat
—I, too, am here again

It's just a thought. There are many possibilities. In a haiku, it's all right to be a part of the subject. It isn't simply a matter of writing about nature, but capturing that sense that we are a part of nature.

Momoko had added Nature, in the form of the seasonal phrase *ducks arriving*, and Time, with the reference to my returning. Perhaps Nature and Time were related. I read her version, and my mind wandered back to the feelings I had when I first composed it: my exhaustion from working on North Korea, my sense of powerlessness over events, and the calm that settled upon me as I contemplated the duck's webbed feet moving below the surface of the water.

Then Momoko did go, adding as I walked her to the elevator, *Oh, I meant to tell you: your duck haiku, it rightfully remains yours. What I have done with it, we call* tensaku. *It's a kind of poetic editing.*

I went back inside the apartment and looked at my haiku on the dining room table. She was right; only eight of my original seventeen syllables survived the afternoon intact.

four

PUNGENT GRASS, DELICATE WATER

Early in our marriage, my husband and I decided we would split the chores fifty-fifty. I would do half the housework, and he would do half the housework. I would cook three nights a week, and he would cook three nights a week (and to show how flexible we were, we would wing it on the seventh night). As children came along, and I went back to work, we threw our political correctness out the window and settled into an arrangement that worked perfectly well for us. It was a typical 1950s marriage, we joked, but in reverse. My husband raised the children and I went off to work. He did the cooking and cleaning, kept track of vaccination records, and got the kids off to school. Sometimes he taught English part-time, but mostly he spent his free time reading and studying ancient Greek and Latin. (*Someone in this world has to devote himself to reading!* he would say when asked if he might someday write a book.) In the evenings, I would go over the children's homework. On weekends, my husband would escape to Tokyo's used-bookstore district, while I explored different parts of the city with our children. Riding the subways was one of my favorite pastimes, and by the time we left Japan, the children, who spoke little Japanese, could mimic with perfect pitch the many Tokyo train announcements—*Watch your step. Next stop, Ueno Station. Please don't forget your belongings.*

I was going over homework with my daughter when the phone rang.

It was Dr. Mochizuki, the founder of the Numamomo haiku group, on the phone. I was the first non-Japanese member of Dr. Mochizuki's haiku group, and he felt he had an important role to play in my haiku upbringing. He wanted me to know as much as possible about haiku and Japanese culture, and so he wrote or called me frequently. I had gotten to know Dr. Mochizuki over the several months since I joined the Numamomo haiku group. He was an energetic man in his mid-seventies who loved life and good food. During one of our phone calls, I desperately flipped through a Japanese-English dictionary, the phone jammed between my ear and my shoulder, as Dr. Mochizuki tried to describe himself to me, using words like Greek and philosophy and food. I finally found the word in the dictionary and realized he was trying to tell me he was an epicurean. In addition to being a successful Numazu doctor, Dr. Mochizuki published essays on Japanese history and culture. When, at the age of seventy, he started writing haiku, he created his own group.

Dr. Mochizuki was hard of hearing and had the habit of shouting into the phone, thinking that others must suffer from the same ailment. This evening, he shouted: *Abigail-san, you need to come to Numazu and taste really fresh sushi! What you find in Tokyo these days is terrible!*

I was in despair over my daughter's homework. Martha was very bright, but a daydreamer. When I was a child, I always tried to figure out what people wanted of me, and then sought to meet that expectation. But Martha was like Eric, her father, and she went about her life oblivious to the world's expectations. This made her a fascinating human being, but an uneven student. I both despaired of and admired my daughter. If only she would do things my way, I thought, everything would be fine.

Talking to Dr. Mochizuki reminded me that I was having no more luck with my haiku than with my daughter. I had done everything Momoko had asked. But even after my tutoring session, no one was choosing my work at our haiku group. I was no closer to figuring out how to write haiku that were "true to myself" than when I first showed up in Numazu.

Dr. Mochizuki, my haiku are not progressing! I will never be able to write good haiku!

He dismissed my frustration. *You feel disappointed? What about me? A published essayist and a doctor, yet still without a haiku worthy of praise!* He was right. I now recalled that no one had chosen any of his haiku at our last session either. A haiku by Buson came to mind:

行く春や選者をうらむ歌の主
yuku haru ya senja o uramu uta no nushi

spring is passing—
the author of the unselected poem
resents the selector

BUSON

Dr. Mochizuki shouted into the phone, *You need a haiku name! Come to Numazu at seven A.M. this Saturday and I will take you to a place that has the freshest sushi in all Japan! And we'll get you a haiku name!*

A week later I was standing on the docks of Numazu, shivering in the cold, watching fishing boats bob against the pier. Dr. Mochizuki arrived, impeccably dressed as usual in a three-piece suit, and we walked past fishing nets and drying seaweed to a ramshackle sushi bar just off the pier.

We entered the bar, letting the warped screen door swing shut behind us. Dr. Mochizuki told me it was here among weary fishermen and small shopkeepers that he ate breakfast every morning before going to his hospital.

We sat at the sushi bar facing a lanky, leathery-skinned man in a white apron. The man nodded to Dr. Mochizuki, scooped up some rice, and patted it in the palm of his hand. His hands moved quickly. He smeared a dab of *wasabi* on the rice and topped this with a thick moist slab of tuna extending far over the ends of the sticky rice. We drank our miso soup and watched the sushi chef at work.

My lack of progress in writing haiku made me all the more eager to get a haiku name. At least on the outside, I thought, I would seem more like a haiku poet. Bashō had had at least three haiku names in his lifetime; Bashō was the last. He chose this name because it was a type of banana tree of which he was fond, given to him by a student. The haiku name of another famous poet, Issa, meant "a cup of tea." I knew that not everyone in the Numamomo haiku group had a haiku name, but those who did had lovely names like Dance, Heart-Snow, Flower in Snow, and Sound of the Tide.

Dr. Mochizuki also seemed to be deep in thought. After a while he mused aloud:

It makes no sense to educate everyone in the same way. Why seek to turn a fisherman into a scholar? Why do we no longer value the work of a craftsman? We ought to value traditions and skills that have been handed down from generation to generation. Society insists that education is mandatory and that everyone should be educated in the same way, but the fisherman is being robbed of his self-respect!

I interrupted Dr. Mochizuki, and asked him how I should choose a haiku name.

Well, what do you like? he asked.

Oh, I like water—the ocean, rivers, swimming. Something with the character for water, 水, *might be nice. I also love the outdoors and hiking in the mountains. Maybe I could be* sansui, 山水, *mountain water.*

He waved the thought away with his hand. *Too common; it sounds like bottled mineral water!*

What about ryūsui, 流水, *or rushing water?* I asked.

Too male. Why don't you try tansui, 淡水, *light, delicate water, instead?*

I had mixed feelings about taking such an ethereal name. Somehow it did not match my self-image. I wanted something more forceful, more daring.

Dr. Mochizuki took a pen and paper from his breast pocket and wrote the Chinese characters for "delicate water." *Good. Now, for a last name. What are some of your earliest memories?*

Dr. Mochizuki surprised me, as I did not know haiku poets had haiku last names. In fact I was sure they did not. But I was reluctant to challenge the founder of our haiku group, and I told myself that maybe Dr. Mochizuki found the sound of my real last name too harsh to the Japanese ear.

My earliest memories? I asked, distracted. I recalled my childhood in Maryland, the stifling humidity of summers without air conditioning, the *click* and *snap* of an aluminum screen door slapping shut on a summer day, the drone of lawnmowers in the neighborhood. *The scent of freshly cut grass, that's one of my earliest memories!*

Grass? That's perfect. Beaming with satisfaction, Dr. Mochizuki wrote down 香草 淡水 . *Kasō Tansui. Pungent Grass, Delicate Water. This is an excellent haiku name for you!*

I looked at what he had written. The Chinese characters were quite beautiful and not too difficult to write. I could practice them at home. But I was still skeptical about having a haiku last name. If I dropped the last part of the name, I would be left with Delicate Water, which did not sound quite like me either. I was uncomfortable with my haiku name, but did not know how to broach this with the self-assured Dr. Mochizuki.

I asked Dr. Mochizuki to tell me his haiku name and how he chose it.

Traveling Man Tree and I were sitting with Momoko in Numazu one day. We were just starting up the Numamomo haiku group and we were discussing our plans for the group. We needed haiku names. I chose Sound of the Marsh because the character for marsh is "numa," *which is the first Chinese character in the name of the town of Numazu, a town that is important to me. Your haiku name should mean something to you.*

Traveling Man Tree needed a name, too. In his case, Momoko chose to name him ryojinboku, *which is a kind of palm tree, tall, with leaves stretching up and out like a giant fan. It is also a term for the staff that pilgrims carry on their journeys. At that time Traveling Man Tree was commuting from Tokyo to Numazu regularly for work, so a haiku name that referred to travel was clever. Also, he was just starting to write haiku, so you might say that he was embarking on a poetic pilgrimage.*

The sushi bar had thinned out as we talked. The morning shift was over and someone was sweeping the floor around us. It was time to go, and I thanked Dr. Mochizuki for helping me find a haiku name. Once outside, Dr. Mochizuki bowed to me and then turned to walk to his hospital. Mulling over my new name, I walked along the road toward the bus stop to catch the bus that would take me to the train station.

I had come to Numazu to get a haiku name. Now I had one that I did not like. Kasō Tansui. Pungent Grass, Delicate Water. It simply did not fit me. I also did not think I should have a haiku last name. To make matters worse, Dr. Mochizuki had said that Momoko had chosen Traveling Man Tree's name. Now I wished Momoko, a haiku master, had chosen my name. But it was too late.

Kasō Tansui. Pungent Grass, Delicate Water. I repeated the name to myself as I walked. Well, perhaps the name was not so bad after all. It did have an elegant ring. And hadn't Bashō used three haiku names in his lifetime? Perhaps a time would come when I would get a new name too.

five

NEW YEAR'S DAY AT ASAKUSA SHRINE

It was late December, the sky had turned a cold gray, and everywhere in the city people were getting ready to observe the centuries-old *o-shōgatsu*, or New Year, seasonal traditions. Homemakers stocked up on *mochi*, round cakes of pounded sticky rice, to place in their homes as offerings to the gods. Shop owners adorned their store entrances with good-luck symbols of pine and bamboo. Even the most anarchic-looking youth in black stopped at shrines to pick up fortunetelling messages and to ring the bell to wake the gods.

But North Korea–related events were casting a pall on the mood in Japan that year. I was spending long evenings at the office trying to convey the complicated picture to Washington. North Korea had begun refueling one of its nuclear power reactors, another step down the path of developing nuclear weapons. At the same time, the Japanese public was seething with anger at North Korea. After having admitted to kidnapping Japanese citizens and forcing them to live in North Korea for decades, North Korea had let some of the kidnap victims return to Japan. The nightly news had played and replayed pictures of them slowly getting off the plane, as if out of a time machine. Now the North Korean government wanted them back, insisting they had only been freed temporarily! To Americans, all this must have seemed a strange and surreal sidebar to the more important nuclear issue. But in Japan, the public was angry. North Korea's nuclear moves were abstract and could not compare to the stories of the kidnapped, including some who had disappeared, never making it back to Japan. I wondered whether my colleagues in Washington, when they read my reports, felt I had gone totally native for explaining in such detail the ins and outs of the kidnapping issue when the nuclear crisis loomed so large.

More and more I found myself turning to haiku for relaxation. With my work, I always seemed to doubt whether I was doing enough. I would watch events unfolding in North Korea and feel that observing and recording was insufficient, that there must be some action I could take to fix the situation. With haiku, however, capturing the thing itself was the goal. The more I accepted the world around me as it was and just described what I saw, the more authentic my haiku.

The New Year season was rich with poetic motifs, so rich that my *saijiki* listed it as a separate, fifth season. *O-shōgatsu* seasonal words included many "firsts," from first calligraphy writing of the year to first dream and first cry of a child. People often greet each other, early in the New

Year, with *hatsuyume o mita?* Did you have a first dream?
A happy first dream is considered auspicious. I was hope-
ful that I would find, or maybe dream, something to write
about.

Momoko had agreed to meet with me early in the
New Year, and I wanted to write as many New Year–
related haiku as possible beforehand. With this in mind I
went with my children by subway to Ueno, one of Tokyo's
oldest quarters, on the afternoon of New Year's Eve. The
train was packed with holiday shoppers. Overworked rail
employees at Ueno Station waved their arms in the di-
rection of the exit as we got off the train, and shouted at
the crowd to keep moving. A befuddled person stood still
among the horde. Under a low, dimly lit ceiling, we shuf-
fled along with the crowd toward the stairs. I was sure that
there was a haiku somewhere in this scene, but nothing
came to mind.

We spilled out onto Ameyayokochō, a bustling street
deriving the first two syllables of its name from "America."
In the immediate postwar period, during the U.S. Occu-
pation, hundreds of black-market stands had dotted the
neighborhood. It was not hard to imagine decommissioned
Japanese soldiers, dispirited and disowned, sleeping in the
station. I had seen decommissioned soldiers wandering the
streets of Banja Luka, Bosnia, in the winter of 1995, after
the end of the Balkan War. I paused, vainly hoping that a
haiku about decommissioned soldiers might emerge.

In front of one shop, two substantial, ruddy-faced
middle-aged women stood behind a folding table, with

boxes stacked high in front of them. A long line of people waited in the cold, stamping their feet, to buy their freshly made *toshikoshi soba*, or special long noodles, a dish eaten with family late on New Year's Eve and symbolizing long life. We joined the line and, as we waited, a haiku came to me. I took off my gloves, opened my notebook, and wrote:

上野駅年越し蕎麦遠い日本
ueno eki toshikoshi soba tooi nihon

Ueno Station
toshikoshi soba
in far Japan

I checked my pocket dictionary. *Toshikoshi soba* was a seasonal phrase. My haiku had seventeen syllables. It was not in the five-seven-five structure (it was five-six-six), but perhaps my haiku group would accept it anyway. To me, I had come up with a haiku, and this was progress. I generously bought four boxes of noodles from the women at the folding table. Sam, my youngest, asked if he could buy candy, and I said yes. For the rest of the morning as we walked around Ueno, I tinkered, distracted, with the haiku in my head.

Back home, my children ran for the computer, pushing to see who would get there first, and I threw myself on the couch, exhausted from the crowds and the cold. I thought of all the things I had to get done before the end of the year. About a year ago, I had taken up Japanese calligraphy. Even though I was a novice, I wanted to send out

New Year's greetings with the Chinese character for "luck" hand-painted on each one. My ambitious project was now stalled in mid-course and the cards were lined up in various states of completion on the dining room table. We had been eating dinner elbow-to-elbow on one end of the table for the last two weeks.

I also needed to call my parents the next day. *First phone call.* I sat up and checked my *saijiki*. Just as I had suspected, this too was a seasonal phrase.

父と母にもなんとなく初電話
chichi to haha ni mo nantonaku hatsudenwa

to my mom and dad,
too, somehow
first call of the year

Very pedestrian, I chided myself. But at seventeen syllables, it clocked in as a haiku and it seemed a waste to throw it out.

That evening, boiling the noodles from Ueno, I mulled over another haiku:

鍋の中柔らかきそば年忘れ
nabe no naka yawarakaki soba toshiwasure

in the pot
soft long noodles
forgetting the old year

The next day, we went as a family to Asakusa Shrine to celebrate the Japanese ritual of *hatsumōde*, or "first shrine visit of the New Year." We woke early and took the train to the Asakusa district, which was once Tokyo's cultural core, home to kabuki and burlesque theaters. Even though that neighborhood had lost some of its shine over the years, to me its decline only added to its charm.

The large red gate leading up to the shrine still looked much as it did when Hiroshige captured the wintry scene in his well-known nineteenth-century woodblock print. A light snow was falling. On either side of the main pedestrian walkway vendors hawked their wares, from traditional boxwood combs and *senbei* salted crackers to cheap made-in-China plastic toys. A couple struggled to push their well-bundled child in a stroller through the crowd. Two young women in gorgeous kimono walked along together, soda cans in hand. A homeless man slumped amid cardboard boxes next to a street lamp, sleeping off the sake of the night before. I wrote:

> ホームレス門側に寝て初詣
> *hōmuresu kadogawa ni nete hatsumōde*

> a homeless man
> slumped beside the gate
> —first shrine visit of the year

That night, lying in bed before going to sleep, I opened my *saijiki* and read some haiku about *hatsuyume*, or first dreams of the New Year:

はつゆめの滞空時間永きかな
hatsuyume no taikū jikan nagaki kana

first dream of the year
hovering in the air
long-lasting

NŌMURA KENZŌ (1949–)

初夢のひとりでたどる熊野道
hatsuyume no hitori de tadoru kumano michi

first dream of the year
alone on the path
to Kumano

KURODA MOMOKO

Kumano is the site of one of Japan's most sacred shrines and of many pilgrimages. Momoko's haiku suggested to me the pursuit of haiku as a spiritual endeavor. I was not a particularly spiritual person, but I slipped into sleep thinking of Momoko's haiku, of solitude, and of the spiritual path.

❀　❀　❀

Two weeks into the New Year, I met Momoko after work at the Yamazato restaurant in the elegant Hotel Okura across from the embassy. Although I often went to the Yamazato for business, this was the first time I was meeting someone here unrelated to work. Immediately after suggesting the restaurant to Momoko I regretted it. It was as if I was breaking an invisible rule in which I separated my work self from my haiku.

Momoko had arrived before me and was calmly seated in the lobby wearing her signature *samue*-like outfit, this one of coarse brown silk with a padded lining for warmth. The 1960s-style decor of the Okura hotel fit her well. She cut a dramatic figure among the sea of self-important businessmen jabbering on cell phones, and she made everyone else look out of place.

Momoko and I walked down the stairs to the restaurant and seated ourselves at the tempura bar. A bright-faced young woman in a pink uniform came over and served us green tea. Momoko took her time studying the menu, selecting an assortment of fish and vegetable tempura, sashimi, buckwheat noodles, and rice. I wondered whether it was only the members of my haiku group who were obsessed with good food or whether this was a trait common to all Japanese haiku poets, or perhaps to all Japanese.

As we waited for the food to come, Momoko suggested that since we had already talked about seasonal words, we should go over two other basic elements of haiku: the seventeen-sound, five-seven-five format, and *kireji*, or cut-words. Momoko's mention of three "basic elements" reassured me, as the more I learned about haiku, the less sure I was of what made a poem a haiku. I would puzzle over why some haiku I read had six syllables in the first line or eight syllables in the second, or twenty syllables in all. Often I would see Japanese haiku written in one straight line.

I didn't know whether I was supposed to divide such haiku into three as I read them or read them all in one breath.

The problem had come to a head one day as I was driving through Tokyo. While waiting for the light to change, I saw the following public service announcement on the side of a bus:

おもいやり人に車にこの街に
omoiyari hito ni kuruma ni kono machi ni

sympathy
toward people, toward cars
toward this town

Seventeen syllables. Five-seven-five format. It must be a haiku, I thought. But when I reached the office and repeated the public service announcement to my Japanese coworkers, none of them thought it was a haiku. I knew they were thinking to themselves, *What kind of a lunatic is she?* One tried to break the news to me gently, *It's not a haiku, it's an advertising jingle.*

Well, I know it's an advertising jingle, but still, isn't it an advertising jingle haiku?

It doesn't have a seasonal word, said another.

But lots of haiku these days are written without seasonal words, I said.

I failed to convince them. Everyone discreetly went back to work.

That night at the Yamazato, Momoko helped me understand why I had been the only one at the office to mistake the jingle for a haiku. *The seventeen syllable, five-seven-five structure is an essential element of haiku, but it is also true that this pattern is a natural rhythm of the Japanese language. Haiku, like all poetry, is sensitive to the rhythm of language. As the five-seven-five structure is quite common in Japanese, it is familiar and pleasing to our ear.*

Momoko was always careful to give me all sides of a matter, perhaps out of concern that I might not have access to the variety of haiku resources available in Japan. She wanted me to learn as much as possible about haiku, even more than she wanted me to learn "Momoko's approach" to haiku. So, having emphasized that the seventeen-syllable, five-seven-five structure was natural in Japanese, and was for her one of the three basic elements of haiku, Momoko then talked about other ways of looking at the matter. *Even in Japan poets differ on the importance to haiku of the seventeen-syllable structure. Some reject the limitation entirely, while others recognize a number of exceptions.* Writing haiku where the first phrase is six sounds, or *ji-amari*, it turned out, was common. Some haiku broke more naturally into two phrases, of seven and ten or ten and seven sounds. These were referred to as "two phrases, one haiku." Other haiku read best as a single phrase, not broken up at all. These were called "one phrase, one haiku."

I recently had begun writing haiku in English, in addition to the Japanese haiku I was composing for my haiku group. I was uncertain how much of what I was learning about haiku in Japanese applied to haiku in English. This was especially true with syllables in haiku. When I tried to write a seventeen-syllable haiku in English, counting syllables invariably became a distracting, arduous task. Yet in Japanese counting syllables was simple. All syllables were the same length, one beat. The word "scarf," for example, is considered one syllable in English, but the same word (borrowed from the English) is four syllables, or four beats, in Japanese: *su-ka-a-fu*. It was as if all of the pieces of the puzzle in Japanese were the same size and I could choose whichever piece I wished, almost without thinking. In English, I did not know whether I should be writing to a seventeen-beat rhythm, a seventeen-syllable structure, or perhaps something entirely different.

I asked Momoko whether I ought to use a seventeen-syllable structure in haiku in English. She replied almost with indifference, *Oh, in other languages, other rhythmic patterns might be more appropriate.* After more prodding, she mentioned an approach she had heard was common in English, focusing on a pattern rather than syllables: a short phrase, a longer more substantial phrase, and then another short phrase. I said I had read haiku in English that were written all in one line, and other haiku written in two lines. She nodded and, clearly reluctant to advise me on writing haiku in English, simply stated, *You should ask an English-language linguist or poet what form is best in English. The important point is to seek a natural rhythm in your language, and work your haiku from there.*

As we waited for dessert, Momoko asked me about the haiku I had been working on. I was so absorbed in our conversation that I had forgotten to talk to her about my *o-shōgatsu* haiku. I wrote out my haiku about noodles, then explained the context:

鍋の中柔らかきそば年忘れ
nabe no naka yawarakaki soba toshiwasure

in the pot
soft long noodles
forgetting the old year

When I thought of this haiku, I was in the kitchen cooking New Year's noodles. It was dark outside and nice and warm in the kitchen. My children were playing a board game in the next room. My husband was upstairs, arranging his books. I was happy that we were all relaxed and that we would all be sitting down together to enjoy our meal. It is rare that I cook dinner, and that, too, felt different. Usually it's my husband who does the cooking. So I was happy that I had bought the long noodles and was cooking dinner that evening.

Momoko took the white cardboard coaster from under her water glass and wrote:

湯であげて年越しそばを一家して
yu de agete toshikoshi soba o ikka shite

bringing to a boil
New Year's noodles
making a home

It's just a thought. We could probably work on this one

some more. There is a lot you can do with seventeen syllables.
Think of haiku as the vessel into which you pour your feelings.
When you explained your haiku to me, you talked about your
family. So it is good to try to capture that mood in your haiku.
It isn't just the noodles, but what they evoked for you that is
worth writing about, in this case a feeling of family harmony.

Momoko commented on another of my haiku:

父と母にもなんとなく初電話
chichi to haha ni mo nantonaku hatsudenwa

to my mom and dad,
too, somehow
first call of the year

Here you are writing about calling your family, far away
in America. There is no need to hide that your family is in
America. You can bring out this element directly in your haiku.
Especially after the terrorist attacks on the World Trade Center,
perhaps you worry for your family in America in a different
way. Then, changing the seasonal word from "first call of
the year" to "first day of the year," she wrote:

米国の父母に電話をお元日
beikoku no fubo ni denwa o oganjitsu

calling
my parents in America—
first day of the year

I had always thought that leaving some things unsaid was the mark of a good haiku, yet here was Momoko telling me it was all right to be specific about my parents being in America. I wanted to ask Momoko about this, but she had moved on to a discussion of *kireji,* or cut-words, which she considered one of the three basic elements of haiku. I would have to save my question about specificity and subjectivity in haiku for another day.

Kireji *are easy to grasp,* she said. *These words have no concrete meaning but are sounds that can add emphasis or alter the rhythm of a poem. The most common cut-words are the sounds* keri, kana, *and* ya, *although there are many others, too.*

Sometimes I would find *kireji* translated into English as a dash, an exclamation point, or a comma. Some translators insert the exclamation "Ah" or "Oh!" in the place of a *kireji.* A common phrase in Japanese haiku, for example, is *samusakana* or "the cold *kana.*" By tacking *kana* on to the end, the word "cold" lasts for a full five syllables, or the duration of one line in a five-seven-five haiku.

葱白く洗ひたてたるさむさかな
negi shiroku araitatetaru samusa kana

winter leeks
washed all white
ah . . . the cold!
BASHŌ

Again rejecting the notion that haiku is only about

structure, Momoko said, *A haiku poet has to develop a feel for the use of cut-words.*

磨崖佛おほむらさきを放ちけり
magaibutsu oomurasaki o hanachikeri

from the Buddha carved into a cliff
a giant purple butterfly
set free!

KURODA MOMOKO

Momoko explained her poem to me: *The beautiful giant purple butterfly is Japan's national butterfly. A* magaibutsu *is a stone statue of Buddha carved into a cliff. One spring day, I watched as a purple butterfly flew up from the palm of the Buddha, released as if Buddha himself was flying into the sky.*

I looked at Momoko's use of the word *hanachi*, meaning "to set free," "to liberate," followed by the cut-word *keri*. Both ended in *i*, adding to the rhythm of the poem. *Keri* sounded right to me in Momoko's poem because it had a definite, bold sound, reinforcing the contrast between the hard stone out of which the Buddha is carved and the lightness of the butterfly.

That evening, I had expected Momoko to explain to me the rules of haiku. Instead, while setting out the structural elements of haiku, she also began to redefine my conception of haiku. I had been intent on learning the rules; she was intent on teaching me the feel of haiku. *Think of haiku as the vessel into which you pour your feelings*, she had said. I had approached haiku and my haiku group as an explorer, curious about the jungle. Now Momoko was telling me that I needed to go beyond that. I needed to bring my feelings into writing haiku. I was not at all sure I had it in me to do so. I thought back to the other members of my haiku group, to Field and Stream with her caricature on her calling card, to Traveling Man Tree and his golf hobby, to Dr. Mochizuki in his three-piece suit on the docks of Numazu at seven A.M. They all seemed rather ordinary, if eccentric, people. None of them matched my preconception of the sensitive, reclusive poet. If they could do this haiku thing, then perhaps I could too.

six

FOG ON THE LAKE

When I first began to read Japanese haiku, they seemed to be exotic, cryptic glimpses into the Orient:

猿を聞く人捨子に秋の風いかに
saru o kiku hito suteko ni aki no kaze ikani

to those who lament the cries of monkeys
what of the abandoned child
in the autumn wind?

    BASHŌ

芭蕉忌にビルのガラスの絶壁よ
bashōki ni biru no garasu no zeppeki yo

Bashō remembrance day—
the side of a building
precipice of glass

    YAMAGUCHI SEISHI (1901–94)

伯林の雪にぬらせし手袋よ
berurin no yuki ni nuraseshi tebukuro yo

gloves
wet
with the snow of Berlin
YAMAGUCHI SEISON (1892–1988)

I struggled to understand the meaning of these poems. For a while I convinced myself that the less I understood about a haiku, the more "Japanese" and therefore authentic it must be. Inscrutability was simply one more essential aspect of haiku, along with seventeen sounds, seasonal words, and cut-words. Perhaps all this was somehow linked to Zen—a form of Buddhism brought to Japan in the twelfth century from China— and my difficulty with haiku stemmed from my failure to understand Zen teachings.

Many twentieth-century Western scholars of haiku were convinced that haiku reflected Zen philosophy. R. H. Blyth, a major Western interpreter of Japanese haiku, came to Korea in 1924 and became a devoted student of Zen, reading the works of the famous Zen scholar Daisetz Suzuki. He eventually moved to Japan and spent the war years there interned as an enemy alien. Ironically, it was during his long years of internment that Blyth was able to devote his days to the translation of Japanese haiku that eventually made him famous. After the war, his learning earned him the position of tutor to the Crown Prince and sometime foreign advisor to the imperial court.[4]

When Blyth published the first of his four volumes on Japanese haiku in 1949, he proclaimed that Zen Buddhism was the dominant influence in Japanese haiku. "Haiku are to be understood from the Zen point of view," he wrote in the preface to the first volume of his widely read anthology of Japanese haiku.[5] "What this is may be gathered more or less directly from this volume, and perfectly because indirectly from the verses themselves." I was lost but respectful.

Later Western writers and poets drank of the same elixir. Nearly all of the haiku-related books written in English in the 1950s and 1960s seem to accept the idea that Zen is somehow central to haiku.

I was surprised, then, to discover that no one in my haiku group seemed particularly interested in Zen. I would ask members of our group how Zen inspired their work and get puzzled looks in return. Field and Stream, trying to be polite, simply repeated, *Ah, so desu ka? Is that so?* When I pressed for more, she said she had heard that many Westerners think of haiku as a kind of Zen art. But she could not think of any well-known Japanese haiku poets, except perhaps Bashō, who were deeply affected by Zen. *I suppose that many haiku writers have some sympathy with Zen concepts, especially the connections between nature and human beings and the mind. I guess it might be possible to say that the writing of haiku contains, even if unconsciously, the moment attained by Zen practice. But I don't feel I have any understanding of Zen, and although I write haiku I have nothing to do with Zen.* Field and Stream concluded by reminding me that Zen is not a knowledge but a practice and that what is attained is personal realization. *I've never practiced Zen, but I do practice haiku.*

Sound of the Tide, who had lived in New York for six years and picked up some American habits, was much more direct. *Zen and haiku? For me, Zen has little to do with haiku. The people who do haiku in Japan are different from the group of people who are studying Zen.* Instead, she felt that the brevity of haiku forced a kind of minimalism or restraint. *Haiku is a short poem, with only seventeen syllables. There is no room for long words like "beautiful" or "sympathetic." That's the source of the misimpression in the West that Zen and haiku are linked.* Sound of the Tide argued that inscrutability in haiku is not about Zen, but about the Japanese language. *What Westerners fail to understand is that the Japanese language is inherently ambiguous. We are used to the ambiguity of our language. It feels quite natural for us to read a haiku and see several possible meanings. We like to leave things open, and not tie a meaning down.*

I was reluctant to turn against everything I had read up to now in English about haiku. Perhaps, I reasoned, Zen simply permeated Japanese culture—just as Judeo-Christian values permeate the West. If so, then my haiku friends might unwittingly be composing haiku in a Zen spirit. But this logic did not seem to hold. There was nothing Zen about my haiku friends. It would be as odd to look for Zen motifs in all of Japanese haiku, I decided, as it would be for a Japanese student of Western literature to seek Christian motifs in the works of every Western writer.

One day I asked Momoko what she thought of the connection between Zen and haiku.

She replied, *When I first traveled abroad to give haiku workshops, I was surprised that people asked me to explain Zen philosophy to them. Zen is personally important to me, but Zen is not an essential element of contemporary Japanese haiku. Some haiku writers bring a Zen influence to their poetry, but many, many others do not. The important point is that you bring your own inspiration into the writing of your haiku.*

Momoko's explanation made sense. I knew that Bashō had been a student of Zen, and so it would have been natural for him to bring his personal Zen inspiration into his poetry. Bashō's Zen studies began when he moved to Edo (now Tokyo) at the age of twenty-nine. There he met the priest Butchō, who taught him about Zen.[6]

Many of Bashō's most famous poems do have a mystical, Zen-like quality to them:

古池や蛙飛び込む水の音
furuike ya kawazu tobikomu mizu no oto

an old pond
a frog hops in
the sound of water

But Bashō's poetic gifts and his work in the haiku form predate his study of Zen. Here is a verse by Bashō, written in 1666, when he was just twenty years old, seven years before he took up the study of Zen:

姥桜咲くや老後の思い出
ubazakura saku ya rōgo no omoiide

an old cherry tree in full bloom
fervent feelings of old age

Bashō's haiku may well have been influenced by his subsequent study of Zen, but it does not seem right to say that Zen is essential to haiku or, as some would have it, that haiku sprang from Zen.

Even after his study of Zen, Bashō wrote beautiful poems that were not imbued with the Zen spirit, or at least no more than the poems he wrote in his youth had been:

やまつつじ海に見よとや夕日影
yamatsutsuji umi ni miyo to ya yūhikage

mountain azaleas
seen in the sea—
flaming sunset

For all his association of haiku with Zen Buddhism, R. H. Blyth concedes that Bashō does not appear to have thought that Zen is essential to haiku. Blyth points out that Bashō did not instruct his disciples to practice *zazen* and that he rarely mentioned the connection between Zen and haiku.[7]

But if haiku's sparse, inscrutable element does not come from Zen, then how could I explain it? How else might I unravel the mystery of haiku?

Momoko once gave me a clue when she explained to me the origins of haiku. Originally, she said, haiku was the first verse of a longer poetic form called *renga*, or linked verse. Structurally, *renga* consist of long chains of linked verses, the first one having a five-seven-five-syllable structure, the next a seven-seven, and so on, alternating between these two types of short verses. The opening verse of the *renga*, known as the *hokku*, is considered the most important. It sets the tone and the seasonal context for the entire poem. When Bashō began writing poetry, he followed the tradition of the day, writing linked verse in the company of other poets under the guidance of a master. Bashō's claim to fame, Momoko explained, lies in his freeing of the *hokku* from the rest of the poem. That first verse became poetry in itself.

By making the *hokku* a poem in itself, Bashō bequeathed to us a new form of poetry that by its very brevity makes it accessible not just to a select group of talented poets but to just about anyone who has the impulse to write. But it seemed to me that Bashō's legacy has a downside. The *hokku* lacked the context that linked verse provided, making haiku, at times, "inscrutable."

Bashō seems to have been aware of the "inscrutability" problem, and he did not shy away from finding ways to inject context into his haiku. Some of his most successful writings are his travel sketches, which are a mixture of poetry and prose. Many of his haiku were originally embedded in these travel sketches.

Here is the passage from Bashō's "Records of a

Weather-Exposed Skeleton" in which he includes, and contextualizes, his haiku about a child crying in the autumn winds:

As I was plodding along the River Fuji, I saw a small child, hardly three years of age, crying pitifully on the bank, obviously abandoned by his parents. They must have thought this child was unable to ride through the stormy waters of life which run as wild as the rapid river itself, and that he was destined to have a life even shorter than that of the morning dew. The child looked to me as fragile as the flowers of bush-clover that scatter at the slightest stir of the autumn wind, and it was so pitiful that I gave him what little food I had with me.

> 猿を聞く人捨子に秋の風いかに
> *saru o kiku hito suteko ni aki no kaze ikani*

> to those who lamented the cries of the monkeys
> the abandoned child in the autumn wind
> what of that?

How is it indeed that this child has been reduced to this state of utter misery? Is it because of his mother who ignored him, or because of his father who abandoned him? Alas, it seems to me that this child's undeserved suffering has been caused by something far greater and more massive—by what one might call the irresistible will of heaven. If it is so, child, you must raise your voice to heaven, and I must pass on, leaving you behind.[8]

The tradition of embedding haiku in prose continues to this day in Japan. Momoko once sent me a copy of one of her books, *A Haiku Trek through Famous Sites of Hiroshige's Edo.* This slim volume is a travel sketch of sorts, consisting of various trips—known in the haiku world as *ginkō,* or poetry-writing expeditions—that Momoko and some of her haiku friends had made to places in Tokyo memorialized by Hiroshige in his nineteenth-century woodblock prints of old Edo. As in Bashō's travel diaries, Momoko's book provides the reader with the context that inspired the haiku. In each chapter, she describes in prose how her group approached each place, what it must have looked like in Hiroshige's era, and what it looks like today. Some five or six haiku, written by individual participants on the excursion, follow the prose explanation.

It is also common in Japan to add context to haiku by providing a few interpretive lines following the text. Yamaguchi Seishi, for example, has provided the following commentary to his haiku, cited at the beginning of this chapter:

> Bashō remembrance day—
> the side of a building
> precipice of glass

> *Bashō died near Minami Midō, in Osaka. I attended a memorial service for Bashō and glimpsed the glass wall of the C. Itoh Building towering off to the north. It was a precipice of glass, something unknown to Bashō.*[9]

And Seison's haiku "gloves / wet / with the snow of Berlin" made more sense to me when I read Momoko's annotated version of the text:

The poet is recalling his days as a foreign student in Berlin, over thirty years before. The glove must have been a leather glove. The leather wet with the snow of Berlin. Over the years, the memory held within the glove has become even more vivid. An oft-used man's black glove, and the snow in the background has now been brought to the fore.[10]

Here is another haiku by Seison, composed in 1988, the year he died, and annotated by Kafū, one of his disciples:

願ぎごとのあれもこれもと日は長し
negigoto no are mo kore mo to hi wa nagashi

praying
for this and that
the days grow long

The summer of 1988, he had checked into the hospital for the third time. He wrote this haiku while in a bed in the old people's wing of Tokyo University Hospital. An intern had come around handing out strips of paper for the Tanabata festival [July 7, when people write down wishes or prayers on narrow strips of paper and hang these from bamboo]. *Seison's condition was showing a slight improvement. He wrote two haiku, one on the strip of paper for Tanabata and one on a larger square of paper* [often used for writing poetry]. *This is one of the haiku he wrote. He would always say, "Well, I can't very well stay here forever!"*[11]

When I once asked Momoko to send me a few of her favorite haiku that she had written, she included interpretive notes for each of them.

> 能面のくだけて月の港かな
> *nōmen no kudakete tsuki no minato kana*
>
> a Noh mask
> shattered fragments of the moon
> in the harbor
> > KURODA MOMOKO

The seasonal phrase is "moon in the harbor," which suggests autumn. The harbor was full of moonlight. The moon was reflected in the ripples on the surface of the sea. The moon, mirrored in each ripple, was like the fragments of a Noh mask.

> とぶように秋の遍路のきたりけり
> *tobu yō ni aki no henro no kitarikeri*
>
> as if flying
> toward me comes
> the autumn pilgrim
> > KURODA MOMOKO

*The seasonal word is "autumn pilgrim." The man
bounding toward me has undertaken the pilgrimage
started by the Monk Kūkai to eighty-eight temples on
Shikoku Island. The distance covered by this pilgrimage
totals more than 850 miles. The writer [Momoko] goes
on a pilgrimage four times a year, once for each season.
A young man wearing the white robe of a pilgrim was
coming toward the writer, who was a little tired of
walking, with a big stride, nearly flying. The writer
makes it a principle to create haiku in the field, making
the work quite realistic.*

Providing additional commentary to haiku, I was beginning to understand, is common practice in Japan. Even when the author is not available to provide commentary, a scholar or professional poet might flesh out the interpretation. Makoto Ōoka's commentary on poetry in the popular *Asahi Shinbun* newspaper, translated by Janine Beichman, is perhaps the best known among these.

> 闘鶏の眼つむれて飼われけり
> *tōkei no manako tsumurete kawarekeri*
>
> a fighting cock
> eyes gone, still kept
> still fed
>
> MURAKAMI KIJŌ (1865–1938)

*... Born into a samurai family with an annual
income* of *350* koku, *Kijō contracted ear disease and
for many years worked as a poorly paid scribe at the
Takasaki District Court in order to support his wife
and ten children. He studied haiku with the young
Masaoka Shiki and then with Takahama Kyoshi. In
his style, Kijō confronted life head-on and showed a
rugged individuality. A blinded fighting cock is of no
use anymore. One would expect it to be killed, but out
of pity, its owner still keeps it. The poet sees himself in
the rooster but avoids sentimentality by letting only the
rooster into the poem.*[12]

My preconceptions about haiku were slowly falling away. It was commonplace in Japan to annotate haiku. No one I met suggested that my failure to grasp a certain haiku was because I lacked the Zen spirit. Haiku in Japan is a popular art, practiced by a wide range of people, and meant to be understood. It is not, as I had feared, an exclusive club for the spiritually adept few.

seven

WHITE LEEKS

Early in the New Year, North Korea announced to the world that it was pulling out of the Nuclear Non-Proliferation Treaty. We were in the midst of a nuclear crisis with North Korea, and I was going over to the Japanese foreign ministry on a near-daily basis to get their reading of the situation. At the same time, the other story, that of the kidnappings, was widening in scope. Some had thought that the return of the kidnap victims would put a close to that horrible chapter. But for the Japanese public, it turned out to be just the beginning. For years, rumors of kidnappings were dismissed as the wild imaginings of distraught family members. Now that North Korea had confessed, many Japanese felt betrayed, and more confused than ever. People wondered how many others had been kidnapped and whether there were more victims still languishing in North Korea. Curious as to where all this was headed, I expanded my web of contacts and began meeting with members of ad hoc citizens groups.

It wasn't enough, I felt, to dismiss the kidnapping issue as a human rights matter of secondary importance. I had grown up watching scenes of American diplomats in the late 1970s held hostage in Iran by what had up to then been considered insignificant revolutionary youth. I carried with me the lesson that diplomats need to be out and about, meeting with all kinds of people, not just government-sanctioned elites, and not just with people who we judged shared our priorities. In a coffee shop near the embassy, one member of a group of supporters of kidnap victims gave me a poster they had just put together, profiling over seventy missing Japanese, including some disappearances dating back to the 1940s. Japan's missing, shrouded in anonymity for decades, now had names and faces. We had an obligation to understand what people were feeling.

Perhaps it had been this same desire to reach out, wherever I was, to the broadest possible community that had inspired me to take the train to Numazu many months back and to find out for myself what a haiku group was all about. I was always curious about people and places. As a child, I had a world map in the shape of a plastic inflatable ball hanging from the ceiling. One of my favorite pastimes was to spin the ball with my eyes closed, point my finger at a spot, and then open my eyes to see where I would live when I grew up. I had married a man who shared with me this same thirst for travel and adventure, and so my Foreign Service career worked well for us.

My interest in learning about people permeated everything I did, including what I read. I had recently bought a subscription to the *Numazu Voice*, a newsletter edited by Dr. Mochizuki that included articles and essays written by people who live in the Numazu area. They were people who had nothing to do with making foreign policy, and I wanted to know what ordinary people outside the big city of Tokyo were thinking.

The *Numazu Voice* was a home-grown newsletter. A black-and-white photograph of a wild animal not native to Japan appeared on the first page of each issue, with a caption describing its size, diet, and habitat. On the inside pages were fascinating essays on subjects rarely discussed by Tokyo elites or within diplomatic circles. Often it was the unfinished business of history that was being debated: Should Japan's War Remembrance Day—the day of its surrender to the Allied forces—be referred to as "End-of-the-War Day" or "Day of Defeat"? Had the Education Reforms of 1946 been good for Japan's youth, or harmful? We were in the twenty-first century and there were people in Japan still arguing over changes made a half a century before.

"Momoko's Selection" was a regular feature of the newsletter, listing about ten haiku chosen from Numa-momo haiku group gatherings. It was there, for the first time in my life, that I saw my haiku in print.

Momoko, or perhaps Dr. Mochizuki, had chosen to include a haiku I had written some time back, about cicadas:

窓閉めて七階の部屋蝉時雨
mado shimete nanakai no heya semishigure

window closed,
up to the seventh floor
cascading cries of the cicada

I read and reread my haiku. I was a published haiku poet! Just as Mr. Jourdain in Molière's *Le Bourgeois gentilhomme* discovers one fine day that he has been speaking "prose" all his life, I walked around my apartment beaming with pride. Having my haiku published gave me a sense of legitimacy, a stamp of approval. I might now say to anyone willing to listen, *Oh, yes, I write poetry.* I mouthed the words as I paced around my apartment. I could not wait to write more haiku and get them published.

Many hours later I came back down to earth, but from then on I was hooked. Each month I would push aside the bills, the junk mail, even the letters from friends and family, to reach into my mailbox for that familiar brown envelope of the *Numazu Voice*. Flipping to the haiku page, I would check whether I had been "published" once again.

Later, I learned that hundreds of thousands, if not millions, of amateur haiku writers across Japan were, like me, enjoying the thrill of seeing their work in print. Most haiku groups are linked in some way to a publication, however small, that will print their haiku. Other haiku writers might send their work to a major newspaper, hoping that their haiku will be selected and commented on. Haiku web sites and television programs were also popular in Japan.

I once watched an hour-long program devoted to haiku about the *biwa*, or loquat fruit.

弔問の途中の枇杷が綺麗なり
chōmon no tochū no biwa ga kirei nari

on the way to paying condolences
a loquat tree
has become beautiful
SUZUKI SHINICHI (1957–)

Momoko told me that she started her own monthly journal, *Aoi*, in 1990, after the death of her mentor, the haiku poet Yamaguchi Seison. Until then she had been a contributor to Seison's literary journal, *Kasō*, or Summer Grass. Unlike Dr. Mochizuki's local newsletter, Momoko's magazine was a hefty journal dedicated exclusively to haiku.

Momoko encouraged all of her students to contribute to *Aoi*. She once described *Aoi*'s philosophy as being a magazine "by the readers and for the readers." She did not want it to be a vehicle for her own work or to publish only the poems of a coterie of haiku insiders.

Momoko's principles were unusual in Japan, where it was easy for haiku circles and haiku journals to become—deliberately or not—cults of personality. In the feudalistic, factionalized world of Japanese haiku, Momoko was unusual in not minding at all if her students belonged to several different haiku groups.

Momoko spoke to me about her haiku philosophy one evening over dinner at a restaurant called Yayoi. From the outside it looked like a nondescript hole-in-the-wall, but inside, behind the shabby façade, near-unimaginable beauty reigned. Each course changed with the seasons, and the owner painstakingly wrote each menu by hand on a thin sheet of bark.

I want all of my subscribers to feel that Aoi *is their magazine. We are all equal. After all, a haiku is a piece of one's soul, and all souls should be treated with equal dignity.* Momoko told me she named her magazine for the raw indigo pigment used for centuries as a dye in the making of traditional Japanese blue cloth. It was not just the traditional significance that appealed to her, she said. There was spiritual symbolism as well.

To make the indigo dye, raw pigment is poured into a large crock where the seeds are allowed to ferment. It is this bringing together of various seeds in one crock which allows for the fermentation process. Out of this emerges the stunningly beautiful blue color prevalent in Japanese art. My hope is that by bringing together many, many individual haiku, my magazine might serve as a crucible for something even more beautiful and unique. Indigo is a symbol of life and energy.

Momoko's description of her magazine and its philosophy reminded me of the work of Yanagi Sōetsu (1889–1961), a philosopher and art critic who was a leader in the Japanese folkcraft movement. Yanagi worried that Japan, in its rush to catch up with the West, was neglecting its own local handicraft. He devoted himself to preserving and reviving traditional Japanese crafts. In 1925, he and two of his friends coined the term *mingei*, or the people's art.

Yanagi defined *mingei* as the "art of the common classes." He rejected the art world's focus on refined silk and lacquerware at the expense of everyday crafts. *Mingei* objects are humble and functional. Yanagi scoured the countryside for everyday objects. He found beauty in simple crafts, from pots and plates to cotton kimono and blankets—much as in America we have come to appreciate the beauty of well-worked quilts.[13]

Momoko's haiku often seemed to draw upon humble themes:

白葱のひかりの棒を今刻む
shironegi no hikari no bō o ima kizamu

the white leek
—a beam of light—
now I'll chop it

KURODA MOMOKO

月山の薬草乾く月夜かな
gassan no yakusō kawaku tsukiyo kana

Mount Gassan
medicinal herbs are drying
beneath a moonlit night

KURODA MOMOKO

Momoko's manner of treating members of the Aoi

haiku group with the same respect accorded more famous artists, her deep desire to bring haiku to the people—these echoed Yanagi Sōetsu's vision. There were differences, of course, between Momoko's philosophy of haiku and Yanagi's philosophy of crafts. While the *mingei* movement sought to lessen Japan's attraction to Western ways, Momoko welcomed what she called "world haiku." She was delighted when I joined the Numamomo haiku group, not only for my sake, but because of the new perspective she hoped I would bring to other members of our group. Still, Yanagi and Momoko shared a desire to break down the barrier between artist and disciple, and to call into question society's often mistaken notion of who and what really counts in the world.

2

友愛

yūai

FELLOWSHIP

eight

THE GRAPEVINE TRELLIS

Who were all these people in Japan writing haiku? I had called Traveling Man Tree earlier in the week, hoping he might help answer my question, and he had suggested we meet at Sensōji temple in Asakusa. Now, with the plum blossoms still on the trees and winter giving way to spring, I stood on the steps of the temple, watching Traveling Man Tree slowly make his way through the crowd of sightseers.

Traveling Man Tree was in a pensive mood that day. When I asked whether he had written many haiku recently, he shrugged. *Once the New Year is over, there isn't much to write about until spring. Nature just seems to shut down for several months.*

菊の後大根のほか更になし
kiku no nochi daikon no hoka sara ni nashi

> after the chrysanthemum
> other than the *daikon*[14]
> —nothing
> BASHŌ

We stood at the top of the steps, facing the statue of Kannon, the Goddess of Mercy. According to legend, a pair of fishermen found the statue in the Sumida River over a thousand years ago. Although the statue was only two inches tall, a huge temple had been built around it. It was now one of Tokyo's most famous temples.

I asked Traveling Man Tree why he started writing haiku.

Oh, there was a time when I was doing a lot of traveling for my company. They were sending me to Numazu practically every week. On one of those trips, I began to think I should do more than sit alone in my hotel room in the evenings, so I joined the Numazu cultural society. That's where I met Momoko and Dr. Mochizuki. One day the three of us were eating together and Dr. Mochizuki proposed that with a famous haiku writer like Momoko among us, we should start a haiku group. That's what got me started.

Traveling Man Tree said he did not know the first thing about writing haiku when they started the Numamomo haiku group, and so they geared the new group to novices like him. Now I understood why Traveling Man Tree had invited me to join his haiku group many months back. But I was no closer to finding out what had attracted him to haiku.

Traveling Man Tree threw a coin into the large wooden box in front of the statue of Kannon. *Imagine a temple this size for a statue only two inches tall! You know, people don't think about the statue of Kannon itself when they come here. They just come to the temple because they enjoy it. And then they keep coming back because it adds something to their life and they build up memories.*

We walked back down the steps and took a side street. Traveling Man Tree pointed to a bronze statue for sale in front of a secondhand shop along the way. The statue was of a boy walking along, carrying a load of wood on his back while bent over a book. *That's Ninomiya Kinjirō,* he said, rubbing the statue's head as he stopped to look at it. *Before the war these statues used to be in front of every schoolyard.*

Ninomiya Kinjirō was a nineteenth-century figure revered as a model of diligence and hard work. He was orphaned as a young child, but refused to sell the family farm. Instead, he toiled for years from early in the morning until late at night, until one day he was able to buy the farm back from creditors. Ninomiya Kinjirō became a wealthy man and dedicated himself to developing Japan, creating a movement to promote success through morality and hard work. In the 1930s, long after Ninomiya's death, the nationalist government turned him into a symbol of devotion to the state. I had read that it was at this time that statues of Ninomiya began appearing in schoolyards in Japan. After the war, most of these statues were destroyed, but it was still possible to stumble upon Ninomiya statues in quiet corners of Tokyo and Japan.

Traveling Man Tree lingered before the statue, lost in thought. *You were asking me about haiku before. I still remember the first haiku I learned in school. We had to memorize it for homework:*

柿喰えばかねが鳴るなり法隆寺
kaki kueba kane ga naru nari Hōryūji

as I bite into a persimmon
a bell begins to ring
Hōryūji

SHIKI

*Every schoolchild learns this one because the first three sounds—*ka, ki, ku—*are the first sounds of the Japanese alphabet. He actually had been hearing the bells of another temple, Tōdaiji, but he changed it to Hōryūji, a temple famous for its persimmon trees. I suppose he thought it fit better with his poem that way.*

I was about to ask him whether he thought it was legitimate to forgo realism for beauty in haiku, when he picked up another thread.

There is a poem of mine you selected at one of our Numamomo haiku classes.

被爆後の生命をつなぐぶどう棚
hibakugo no inochi o tsunagu budōdana

after the bombing
life hangs on
to the grapevine trellis
TRAVELING MAN TREE

When the atomic bomb struck, I was thirteen—a seventh grader, just about the same age my granddaughter is now. It was August, and we were on semester break—although in wartime we didn't really get a summer break. We would go to school, but instead of studying, we spent the day helping with the war effort. On the morning of August 6, I woke up not feeling well. I told this to my mother, who said it would be better for me to stay home. She prepared a futon for me facing the garden. It was while I was resting there that the blast came. I was blown to the back of the house but I wasn't injured. At that same moment, my classmates were near the school where they were working to demolish some houses to clear a road and create a firebreak. They were much closer to the center of the blast. Not a single one of them survived. Almost all of my friends died. I only have a handful of friends left from before the war.

Meanwhile, where I was, collapsed houses had caught fire and the flames were approaching fast. So we fled our house in search of a safe spot. I was running, running. We ran to a field of grapes in the outskirts of town and took shelter there. There was no food to eat, and these grapes were hanging above me. I was very, very hungry, and I remember eating the grapes to survive. So that's my haiku.

Another person in our haiku group told me he interpreted this haiku as saying that, despite the destruction of the bomb, nature, in the form of the grapes, survived. Sometimes a haiku will hold more meaning than you think of when you write it.

Traveling Man Tree rarely spoke to me about the bombing of Hiroshima, although his haiku often touched on the subject.

Some haiku teachers probably wouldn't accept a haiku like mine about the bombing, because it is based on memory, and is not a description of something I am seeing now. But Momoko is flexible about this.

I was moved by Traveling Man Tree's words, and I nodded thoughtfully to him, wishing to convey both that I understood the meaning of what he was saying, and that I deeply appreciated his sharing this very personal story with me.

It was now my turn to be lost in thought, and I too instinctively patted the Ninomiya Kinjirō statue on the head. I had lived nearly eight years in Japan, including two in Hiroshima. In all that time, I had never told anyone that my father worked on the Manhattan Project during the war, helping to build the atomic bomb. His intellectual contribution to our country in wartime was a source of great respect in my family. My father was a hard worker and a kind man, the son of Eastern European immigrants, a man whose own father came to America as an orphan and found work as a shoe cutter. No one in Japan ever asked about my father or the war or my family. The older people who experienced the war rarely talked about it with a foreigner, and the younger people never seemed much interested in knowing more about me. I was an American, which was interesting to them, but the idea that I, too, had parents and grandparents and ancestry and family duties did not seem to register. Besides, what was I to say? *Oh, by the way, my father is a nuclear scientist who worked on the atomic bomb during World War II.* No, I was not likely to be the first to broach the subject.

Traveling Man Tree had spent many hours of his life grappling with the meaning of what he had lived through. My father, I thought, had done the same. After working on the Manhattan Project, he had worked throughout the rest of his career as a civil servant on nuclear nonproliferation and the peaceful uses of atomic energy. Was I examining my own life hard enough?

I thought about some of the events in my life: My father had worked on the Manhattan Project; I had lived in Hiroshima; I gave birth there to my oldest son, who I named after my father. I was assigned to Japan when the North Korean nuclear crisis broke. I joined a Japanese haiku group and met Traveling Man Tree, a survivor of the bombing of Hiroshima. I tended to see my life as if all of the events were happenstance, each unconnected to the next.

Even my appraisal of how I came to haiku had an Alice in Wonderland feel to it, as if I had fallen down a hole and discovered haiku. Perhaps I was approaching my life in the wrong way. Perhaps there was a meaning to my life that eluded me because I was not searching hard enough. If I figured it out, I might feel less powerless over the course of events and see the direction my life should take. I longed for a better understanding of my own life.

We continued walking in silence through Asakusa, back toward the subway station. We stopped to watch a young man making bean-paste-filled sweets, pouring the batter into iron molds heated over flames. The iron molds looked older than the man using them. I wondered what was going through his mind as he worked.

Why do I write haiku? Our walk was over, but before we parted, Traveling Man Tree returned to my earlier question. *Sometimes I will look at something or hear something, and a haiku will come to me. Other times, I will think back on something that made a deep impression on me. I've written some essays on the atomic bombing of my town, and I know some people who have written books. It's fairly common, I think, to write about your memories in an essay or a book. But if you write a haiku about your personal experience, it's impossible to express the whole experience. So you have to think about what is the most deeply impressive part—the true essence of the thing or the event—and write about that. In my haiku about the grapevine trellis and the bomb, it was my hunger that I remembered more than anything else. Just a deep, terrible hunger. I feel that I survived thanks to the grapes. I don't think it is wrong to write a haiku about a memory.*

nine

CAMELLIAS IN THE NIGHT

For several months, Momoko had been urging me to make the acquaintance of Professor Kotani, another member of the Numamomo group. Professor Kotani was a professional historian and essayist, a tall, self-possessed woman of refined taste who would have been at home as easily in Paris or London as in Tokyo. I had been told that her husband became ill early in their marriage and that, not knowing how long he might live, Professor Kotani kept working and writing so that she would be ready to provide for herself and their children when the time came. I was intimidated by her intensity and shied away from her. She did not have a haiku name, and I half-assumed she considered them foolish.

One day I finally did muster the courage to approach her. Our class had just ended, and people were putting away the folding tables. Professor Kotani was wearing a beige tailored dress and fine leather shoes. Her hair was swept loosely back into a bun. I hesitated, but felt obligated to Momoko, who had suggested just moments before that I invite Professor Kotani to take the train with me back to Tokyo.

I introduced myself with all the formal Japanese I could muster. *Forgive me for burdening you. Could I be so bold as to make a request? We are both returning to Tokyo this evening. Perhaps, if my presence would not offend, it might be possible to consider the eventuality of our taking the train back together.*

Professor Kotani glared at me, and I felt a pit in my stomach. I knew this was a bad idea. At last she spoke. *What? I can't hear out of my left ear!* I walked around to her other side, bowed low, and repeated my flowery statement. Her straight jaw softened into a smile, and she answered in perfect English. *Why that's a brilliant idea!* She put on her gray wool cape, adjusted her matching beret, and walked briskly toward the door. I grabbed my army-green padded jacket, and trailed behind.

Another member of our group gave us a lift to the train station some twenty minutes away. By the time we arrived, dusk had turned to night. We bought our tickets, went up to the platform, and sat on worn plastic seats in the evening chill. I was tired from a full day of writing and reading haiku. Even if I had wanted to talk to Professor Kotani, I was on the side of her bad ear. I guessed that she was in her early seventies, about the age of my mother. She was shivering, and I worried about her catching pneumonia. Forgetting that I was in Japan where casual acquaintances do not generally touch each other, I put my arm around Professor Kotani, to shield her from the cold. We huddled together in silence, waiting for the train.

The train came into the station and we found seats in a near-empty compartment. I settled myself in next to the window, leaned back, and closed my eyes. I was grateful for the warmth, the return home, and the gentle swaying of the car as it pulled out of the station.

Do you ever wonder about the haiku Momoko does not select to read aloud? I must have been dozing. *Hmmm?* I replied. In fact, it had never occurred to me to think about the haiku Momoko did not select. Mostly, I was thrilled with the haiku she did choose, especially when mine was among them.

Here, look at this one. Professor Kotani showed me a haiku she had written down on her rice-paper notepad.

> わびすけやひねくれ一茶 わび住まい
> *wabisuke ya hinekure Issa wabizumai*
>
> a Chinese camellia
> and the impoverished hovel of
> Issa the twisted

Issa is one of Japan's most beloved poets, a humble man whose life was filled with personal tragedy. He was famous for the simplicity and wit of his haiku that captured scenes of everyday life.

> 大根引大根で道を教えけり
> *daikon hiki daikon de michi o oshiekeri*

> pulling up *daikon*
> he showed us the way
> with a *daikon*
>
> ISSA

I had trouble understanding Professor Kotani's haiku. I found it odd that she would describe the beloved Issa as twisted. Maybe she meant that his tragic life in some way distorted him. Issa's four children all died before the age of two; his wife died giving birth to their fourth child. Issa, who had first married at age fifty-one, remarried, divorced, and married again, but died within two years of his last marriage. His last wife was pregnant at the time of his death. I tried to picture a camellia and Issa's home, but no image came to mind.

I wonder why she did not select my haiku. Professor Kotani was frowning at her poem, speaking almost to herself. *Are you familiar with the term* wabi?

I nodded in response. I knew that the term, sometimes translated as "humble simplicity," reached back hundreds of years to the tradition of the tea ceremony. *Wabi* (along with a companion term *sabi*, akin to loneliness) was a concept embraced by the humble "grass-hut" school of tea led by Sen no Rikyū in the fifteenth century. That school found beauty in simplicity and rejected the extravagant tea ceremonies of the upper classes. For centuries tension reigned between the two philosophies, humble simplicity versus opulence. It was not until Japan opened to the West in the second half of the nineteenth century that the *wabi* aesthetic won out for good.

Two of the words in my haiku, wabisuke *and* wabizumai, *derive from the term* wabi. *A* wabisuke *is a Chinese variant of the common camellia, more delicate, with fewer petals, the rarest of all camellias. By contrast, Issa's humble abode is a* wabizumai. *One word symbolizes opulence, while the other represents humility. My haiku highlights these contrasts.*

Beyond the common root of the word for humble abode and the name of this particular winter-blooming camellia in Japanese, I wondered how Professor Kotani would connect the concept of *wabi* with her haiku. *Did Issa enjoy the tea ceremony?* I asked, somewhat at a loss.

Why, I have no idea! The point is that Issa was writing haiku during this period of tension between the aesthetics of opulence and simplicity, or wabi. *As a haiku writer, he embodied the* wabi *aesthetic. It is fitting that his hovel should be referred to as a* wabizumai, *or a* wabi *living quarter. He lived in poverty all his life.*

She looked at her haiku some more and frowned again. *Of course, it's foolish to take the* wabi *aesthetic to the extreme. I mean, even Issa's cold, damp little shack has the word* wabi *in it and I don't think there was anything exquisite about it at all! It must have been freezing in the wintertime and full of mosquitoes in the summertime. At some point austerity loses its aesthetic value, I should think.*

Many Western authors are convinced that the ideals of *wabi* and *sabi* are essential to haiku. Momoko saw things differently. She once told me that she believed *wabi* had been central to the definition of beauty when Japan's ancient haiku masters were writing, but that the definition of beauty was not static. Standards change, she said. Contemporary haiku writers are composing verse in a different era, and a haiku poet today might choose to draw on the *wabi* aesthetic, but it was hardly a requirement. Momoko regretted that when some people heard mention of haiku, they thought to themselves, *Oh, the aesthetics of* wabi *and* sabi, and concluded that haiku was not for them.

Professor Kotani continued, *Of course, my haiku is a commentary on present-day Japan. After years of lavish spending and the burst of the "bubble" economy of the 1980s, I should think it is worth remembering that the simple* wabi *aesthetic always wins out!*

She fell silent, and I closed my eyes again. I was feeling trapped by her overly intellectual explanations of her haiku. I tried to doze, but my mind kept working. *You know, Abigail, you are not so different from Professor Kotani.* The thought came to me, but I kept my eyes shut. I hated to admit this to myself, even if it was true. For me, too, everything had its logic; I needed everything to fall into a neat structure.

The other day I had proudly come up with this haiku:

トーストにぬる杏のジャム師を想う
tōsuto ni nuru momo no jamu shi o omou

on toast
spreading apricot jam
thinking of my teacher

It struck me as so clever at the time. The character for the word apricot in Japanese can be pronounced *momo*, which is also the first character in Momoko, my haiku master's name. Now I understood that it suffered from the same excessive attempt at cleverness as Professor Kotani's haiku about Issa. It was a clever play on words perhaps, but not a beautiful haiku.

The compartment rocked gently as the train sped through the night. My thoughts wandered from camellias to Issa to work. The problem with Cartesian thinkers is that we are not very good at assimilating feelings into our life or work. I was in a career that hardly encouraged this kind of balance anyway. Early on in my diplomatic career, one of my supervisors quoted with approval some legendary American diplomat (whose name I could not remember) who said that the worst quality a diplomat can have is zeal. I walked around for days fearing I might fall into that ruinous category of "zealous diplomat."

Now, as I dozed, the thought came to me that maybe my problem was the reverse. Maybe I was not zealous enough. Why wasn't striving for freedom in North Korea being discussed more widely?

Professor Kotani woke me from my reverie. *Well, here's another aspect of it: Issa, though humble in his ways, wrote haiku as beautiful as the rarest of Chinese camellia!*

She sighed, *Perhaps I have put too much intellectual rumination into this poem. Yes, now I see it. My haiku lacks spontaneity. It lacks the sensibility of a really good haiku.* Satisfied that she now saw the flaw in her haiku, she closed her notepad, put it back in her bag, and snapped the bag shut.

Our train was pulling into Tokyo Station. We collected our belongings, got up, and moved toward the exit. Just before we got off the train, Professor Kotani turned to me. *Pungent Grass, Delicate Water—why, that is a very odd haiku name indeed! Who gave you that name? Was it Dr. Mochizuki? I suspect it was. You had better change your haiku name. You need something more dignified, something that does justice to your intellect and your background. Abigail was one of King David's wives, you know. You shouldn't throw out your first name so lightly. Good evening.*

So much for the Japanese reputation for subtlety and indirection! I watched, speechless, as this remarkable woman in a gray wool cape and gray beret stepped off the train and commanded her way through the crowd, toward the turnstile. She hardly fit the traditional mold. Maybe this was why Momoko wanted me to meet her. Or perhaps Momoko had decided the time had come for me to meet myself in Professor Kotani.

ten

THE DRAGONFLY

I began studying Japanese calligraphy even before hai-
ku, as a way to improve my Japanese writing skills. On
Wednesday evenings, I would push my way past the dis-
solute bars of Tokyo's Roppongi district, past the loitering
crowds of young girls with pink hair and platform boots,
and head toward the Azabu Jūban area. My calligraphy
teacher, a graceful, elderly woman in her mid-seventies,
lived on the far side of the Jūban, across the narrow Furu-
kawa river. The Furukawa (literally "old river"), like all of
Tokyo's waterways, had lost out in Japan's postwar rush
to catch up to the West. The stagnant river was encased
in concrete. Apartment buildings all along the Furukawa
were built facing away from the water. It was the backside
of life—the trash cans, air conditioners, and outdoor stair-
wells—that communed with the river each day. It was sad
that the Japanese passion for nature in art did not translate
into a day-to-day love of nature itself.

Crossing the river, I followed a narrow street crammed

with small, low houses and dangling telephone wires. Here and there, an apartment had been renovated, adding to the haphazard look of the neighborhood. Early postwar homes of concrete and corrugated tin stood side by side with modern tile and stucco buildings.

My calligraphy teacher, Sugiyama-sensei, had lived in this neighborhood for years. Her home was once a traditional Japanese wooden house with tile roof, sliding doors, and a wooden porch running all along the outside. Some time in the 1960s, partly for profit and partly to enjoy modern conveniences, the house was torn down, and three separate apartment units went up in its place. Instead of a porch, a small recessed square of poured concrete now greeted visitors. Behind my teacher's home, an enterprising neighbor had calculated that he could make four thousand dollars a month by turning his small plot into a parking lot. Sugiyama-sensei kept the metal blinds shut to block out the view.

I opened the rusty gate, careful not to knock over a row of thirsty plants languishing in plastic pots. Next to the pots were sandbags, on hand to protect the front entry from flooding during the rainy season. I rang the bell and pushed the door open slightly.

Dōzo, irasshaimase! Welcome, please come in. My calligraphy teacher greeted me with a kind smile, a bow, and an inviting nod of the head. I took off my shoes and stepped into a cramped hallway stacked to the ceiling with calligraphy magazines, rice paper, and scrolls in torn cardboard boxes. Three large, dusty, gilt-and-marble calligraphy trophies languished atop an old wooden bookcase.

The robust scent of ink filled the air. I followed Sugiyama-sensei into the only room on the ground floor, where low Formica-top tables formed an H in the center of the room. A metal sink for cleaning brushes stood along one wall, and adjacent to that was a large white board. A calendar featuring Japanese poetry composed by members of the imperial family hung on another wall. This month's picture showed the now-deceased Emperor Hirohito and his wife standing on tatami mats, gazing out through a sliding glass door at the garden beyond.

わが庭に冬はきぬらし石垣の蔦のもみじのいろはさえたり

waga niwa ni fuyu wa kinurashi ishigaki no
tsuta no momiji no iro wa saetari

In our garden
winter seems to have come
on the stone fence
ivy leaves
of bright color

In the remaining free space on the walls, Sugiyama-sensei had hung samples of her calligraphy master's work, including a poem painted on a rock the size of my palm, a portion of a Buddhist prayer, and a Bashō haiku:

若葉して御目の雫ぬぐはばや
wakaba shite onme no shizuku nuguwa baya

fresh young leaves
from your eyes, teardrops
wiped away
BASHŌ

Even after a year of studying calligraphy with Sugi-yama-sensei, the Bashō haiku was indecipherable to me, a swift jumble of characters strewn across the page. Seeing me puzzle over it, my calligraphy teacher read it aloud to me and explained its meaning.

Bashō wrote this during a visit to a temple where he saw a wooden sculpture of a famous Chinese sage in tears. The sage had come to Japan and died without ever having the chance to return to the land of his birth. The statue was surrounded by lush, young foliage. Perhaps it was seeing the foliage and thinking of his own youth that had brought tears to the spirit of the sage. Perhaps Bashō was thinking of his youth, too, when he wrote this haiku, as Bashō also was unlikely to return to his childhood home. Bashō imagined wiping away the tears of the statue as he would wipe away his own tears.

It was in this room where Sugiyama-sensei taught students of all ages, but mostly young children. *I love teaching them, because of the sweetness of their souls,* she once said to me. Using big, colorful magnets, she posted their work on the white board. I never met these young children, but I felt that I knew them through their work. Hiro-kun, a six-year-old boy, was working on the word *kome*, meaning "rice." He wrote in thick, bold brushstrokes that filled the white paper with this one tasty word. I imagined Hiro-kun as a happy, confident little boy. Ichirō-kun, another first grader, had written *hikari,* or "light." I pictured him as tall, and perhaps a bit more serious than Hiro-kun. Keiko-chan, a fourth grader, was working on the phrase *mushi no gasshō,* "a chorus of insects." She wrote with a more self-conscious, thin stroke, leaving large amounts of white space on the page, revealing perhaps the first sign of self-doubt.

As with haiku, calligraphy in Japan is taught by do-ing. I had been taking calligraphy lessons with Sugiyama-sensei for about a year. I would come to her home one evening a week and painstakingly copy pages from a cal-ligraphy journal of ancient Chinese masters onto sheets of brown rice-paper. The first time I came to Sugiyama-sensei's home for a lesson, she set out ink, rice paper, and a brush, and asked me to choose a page to copy. I had never held a brush before, but Sugiyama-sensei waited for me to ask her how to hold it before showing me. It was unnerv-ing at first, but over time I understood that when the study has no end, it is the only method that makes sense. As with haiku, one never really "graduates" from calligraphy classes.

Sugiyama-sensei's previous student, a chubby junior high school girl, was just finishing up, and she made room for me at the low table as she put her things away. Dressed in a blue sailor-dress school uniform and bulky white cot-ton leg warmers, the girl was indistinguishable in appearance from thousands like her hanging out in the trendy Shibuya shopping district. But this one was spending her Wednesday evenings brush in hand, carefully copying the works of ancient Chinese masters. Despite her efforts to conform, her originality was coming through.

I unrolled my brushes from the red woven bamboo case and settled into my work, bending back the tip of my brush a few times to soften it and then pouring black ink from a large yellow plastic bottle into a concave slate. I looked up again at Hirō-kun's "rice" character on the wall.

I imagined Hirō-kun's mother as full of devotion, bringing her son to calligraphy classes, preparing him to become the Japanese version of a Renaissance Man. She probably dreamed of his growing up and getting a job at a bank or as a bureaucrat. But she also would want him to be able to compose beautiful Japanese poetry, delicately set down on rice paper in his fine calligraphy.

I berated myself for not having pushed my children more. I had taught them how to take the subways by themselves and had given them the freedom to explore Tokyo on their own. I wanted them to be independent and confident. Somehow piano lessons, calligraphy classes, and even soccer had fallen by the wayside. My oldest son, Abe, was now in eleventh grade and needed to start thinking about applying to colleges. It seemed to me that he needed something to show for all of his years living overseas, seven of which were in Japan. I knew that my career moves put him in a difficult position, as he would be starting his senior year in a new school and in a new country.

Earlier that evening, over dinner, I had tried to en-
gage him on the subject. *Abe, you can't expect to get into a
good college based just on your grades. You need to come up with
something that will distinguish you from others. Why don't you
try writing haiku?*

Our two other children looked at Abe in anticipation.
My husband shook his head.

Seriously, I continued, *smart kids are a dime a dozen.
A kid who has lived in Japan for eight years and has nothing
to show for it . . . I mean, really, it would be embarrassing.* I
asked my son, *What have all of your years living in Japan
meant to you? What do you think is the best thing about Ja-
pan?*

Ramen, he answered.

*Ramen? You can't get into college telling people you like
ramen!*

*Well, I like the ramen here. I like the broth. I like the noo-
dles. I like how it steams up my glasses when I look down into
the bowl. I have fun going with my friends to the ramen shop
at lunchtime. They make good ramen in Japan.*

Abe was our oldest but I had already learned as a
mother that a fifteen-year-old cannot be coerced into any-
thing. Actually, a fifteen-year-old can be coerced, but the
process does far more damage than good. I made a half-
hearted second run, *Aren't you at all curious about haiku?
Doesn't it interest you that I spend so much time working on
haiku?*

*No. You like it and I'm happy for you. But please don't
make me write haiku.*

Leave the kid alone, my husband said as he cleared the table. *Ah, the joys of parenting!* I thought to myself.

*   *   *

I soaked my calligraphy brush in ink and placed black stroke after black stroke on the coarse brown rice-paper as a warm-up exercise. I practiced: top to bottom, left to right, little curls and lines and circles, and then a stroke like a horse's tail. Starting from the upper left, I pulled the brush gradually down to the lower right, letting the stroke become slower and fatter at the bottom until I ever so slowly pulled the brush to the right, up and away from the page.

On evenings like this one when we were alone, my calligraphy teacher and I talked as we worked. I liked these talks almost as much as doing calligraphy itself. This evening I told Sugiyama-sensei that I was getting help from Kuroda Momoko with my haiku. *Oh, you are very lucky,* she replied. *Momoko's haiku are fresh, simple, and clear. I've seen her on television many times. She has an attractive character.*

With her mind now also on haiku, Sugiyama-sensei departed from our usual routine of working from a calligraphy journal. Choosing one of the fatter bamboo brushes, she dipped it in the orange ink she used for teaching and wrote out a haiku:

萩さけり浅間をのぼる雲みだれ
hagi sakeri asama o noboru kumo midare

bush clover in bloom—
climbing Mount Asama
clouds scattering

MIZUHARA SHŪŌSHI (1892–1981)

Sugiyama-sensei's haiku seemed uneven and sloppy. The characters for "bush clover in bloom" were thin and off to the side, while those for "clouds scattering" were almost falling over each other. The word "cloud" itself was much larger than the other characters, and "climbing" was overwhelmed by "Mt. Asama." The last line trailed off at an angle. I worried that my teacher was getting old.

I was wrong.

When a calligrapher writes a haiku, the writing should reinforce the meaning of the text. Look at how I have written Shūōshi's haiku. "Bush clover in bloom" is bunched up the same way clumps of bush clover often are in nature. "Mount Asama" is large and imposing. It was difficult work for Shūōshi to climb up Mount Asama. By using a thick, strong stroke, I reinforce the sense of exertion needed to climb up the hill. Shūōshi is quite exhausted when he gets toward the top of the hill. So he stops to catch his breath. And then, he looks up and, with a feeling of exhilaration, watches the low, heavy clouds overhead breaking up and moving swiftly. Do you see why I have written it this way?

I looked at her work again. Now, I saw not ragged ink strokes but a landscape. It was a landscape with no landscape, a symbol of a landscape.

My teacher's visual explanation of Shūōshi's poem reminded me of e. e. cummings. I had always considered e. e. cummings a superficial poet, someone whose poems are taught to junior high school students because they are visually entertaining. Now it occurred to me that he had been striving for the same visual effect in Western poetry that my teacher was explaining in Japanese haiku.

I went back to my brush, dipping it again in the ink before I, too, tackled the poem. My teacher commented on my work. *You might want to leave a space between the first line and the last two—a pause for emphasis. It's more beautiful that way, don't you think? Writing poetry is a visual art too.*

That Bashō haiku on the wall—it isn't just the poem that is important, but how it is presented.

As we worked in the evening quiet, I asked Sugiyama-sensei whether she had ever composed her own haiku. She picked up another brush before answering, dipping this one in black ink, her words flowing to the rhythm of her brush.

I used to write haiku before the war. We would gather at my friend's house just up the street from here. There were several of us. We would do calligraphy together, and sometimes we would write haiku or tanka [verse in five-seven-five-seven-seven form]. *Some nights we would spend hours just reading haiku and tanka aloud. It all stopped, of course, when the war broke out.*

She had written:

> 春風や闘志いだきて丘に立つ
> *harukaze ya tōshi idakite oka ni tatsu*
>
> spring wind,
> fighting spirit
> standing thus on the hill
>   TAKAHAMA KYOSHI (1874–1959)

I wondered what memories were going through my teacher's head. *Did the government ban haiku gatherings?* I asked, thinking of stories I had read of haiku writers being arrested and thrown in jail during the war for writing what the nationalist authorities considered subversive poems.

No, I was too young to be part of a serious group of haiku poets. We stopped our gatherings because of the firebombing. We couldn't have any lights on in the evening as they might have attracted the planes. And we were afraid of dying all at once, in one place. During the firebombings, many houses right in this neighborhood burned to the ground. Especially up the street, just over the Furukawa river. Many, many people died in this neighborhood.

She picked up her brush again and wrote out another haiku:

> から松はさびしき木なり赤とんぼ
> *karamatsu wa sabishiki ki nari akatonbo*

> the larch
> alone
> but for a dragonfly
> KAWAHIGASHI HEKIGOTŌ (1873–1937)

When I was a young girl, I used to love Hekigotō. He seemed so modern and free.

Today, when I see young girls with boyfriends, it fills me with joy. When I was young, during the war, there were no boys for us to fall in love with.

I had worked on the Shūōshi haiku for over an hour, at times stopping to practice a single stroke on another sheet until I got it right. It was nearly ten in the evening and time for me to get home. I got up to rinse my brushes in the sink, hobbling a bit from sitting in a kneeling position for so long. Sugiyama-sensei went back to talking about haiku.

We often focus on the basic rules of haiku—seventeen sounds and a seasonal word. But Hekigotō refused to limit himself to seventeen sounds. Today many haiku writers do not even use seasonal words. Haiku is very free. Maybe that is why we teach haiku to young children.

Outside, someone was walking by, clapping two thick wooden sticks together. The first time I heard that sound I thought it came from a nearby shrine, but Sugiyama-sensei explained that it was a neighborhood warning for people to put out any fires—nowadays meaning heaters, stoves, and the like—before going to bed. The tradition apparently stretched back hundreds of years, to a time when Japanese homes were made out of wood and people cooked over open fires. Houses were still very close together today, and volunteers still took turns making the rounds, maintaining the tradition.

After an evening doing calligraphy, my mind was as limp as the body after a good massage. Ideas were floating pleasantly in my head. So many traditions live on in Japan, yet haiku is constantly evolving. In a society that prizes order and conformity, haiku seems remarkably revolutionary and free. There is no term in Japanese for the "way" of haiku, as there is for the "way" of calligraphy, the "way" of martial arts, or the "way" of dance. Perhaps this is one reason so many people in Japan enjoy writing haiku.

eleven

MR. FUKATSU'S BASHŌ

*How has Bashō changed my life? Well, it's hard to say. I suppose
I myself would not be able to see this. What impresses me is how
Bashō threw everything else in his life overboard for the sake
of haiku. He wanted to write haiku in an idealistic way. To
do this, he got rid of all of his worldly possessions, left his fam-
ily and friends behind, and set out on his travels. That's how
he wrote one of his most famous works,* Narrow Road to the
Interior. *He even sold his home! I've read many theories about
why he did this. One is that he needed the money to be able to
afford his travels. Another theory is that he really expected to
die during his travels, so why would he need a home? Bashō
staked his whole life on writing haiku. The key to understand-
ing Bashō is understanding his way of life.*

I first learned of Mr. Fukatsu while lying on the couch
at home one evening, studying some of the more obscure
Chinese characters in the haiku in Momoko's magazine,
Aoi. At some point I decided to take a break and read one
of the essays, a much easier task. Someone named Mr.

Fukatsu had written a short article about a class he was teaching on Bashō.

Mr. Fukatsu explained in the article that while he was doing volunteer work at the *Aoi* office one day, Momoko, who also happened to be there, chided him for not doing more with haiku than belonging to a haiku group. She told him to start a study group, on whatever aspect of haiku interested him. Mr. Fukatsu was so surprised by her words that he did not respond. It was only some months later, he wrote, after he won a haiku award and Momoko brought up the idea again, that he began to think seriously about how he might follow her suggestion.

At about the time that Momoko was urging him to do more, Mr. Fukatsu was also reading a book on Bashō he had picked up at a secondhand bookshop. Perhaps he could lead a study group on Bashō. Rereading *Narrow Road to the Interior*, he saw new meaning and richness in Bashō's work. Even though he had no teaching qualifications and no pretensions as a scholar, he decided he would start a study group on Bashō.

Mr. Fukatsu concluded his article by stating that his class met in a public classroom on the fourth floor of the Community Education building in the Kudanshita area in Tokyo. Anyone interested in Bashō was welcome to attend.

I was intrigued. The class met once a month and over the course of a year would read through the entire text of *Narrow Road to the Interior*. Students would read the text aloud, with Mr. Fukatsu providing commentary, based on his extensive reading. I knew of people in the West who worked through Shakespeare's plays with the same passion, and I once participated in a marathon public reading in Paris of the entire text of *The Three Musketeers* by Alexandre Dumas. Somewhere in Tokyo, people were approaching Bashō with this same energy. I went to a bookstore the next day and bought the assigned text. A week later, I showed up for class.

Mr. Fukatsu looked like an old-time Socialist Party worker. I guessed he was in his mid-sixties. He had thick glasses and a salt-and-pepper beard, and he wore a blue denim shirt and well-worn jeans. He sat quietly facing his class, a group of about twenty eclectic Japanese women about his age who were all smiles and ready for some intellectual fun.

Like all dedicated teachers faced with a new subject and new students, Mr. Fukatsu had prepared extensively for his class. He gave us handouts: maps of Japan with wobbly lines marking where Bashō's journeys had taken him, a Chinese calendar with a detailed explanation showing how to convert the days and years in Bashō's text to the modern calendar, and a chronology of Bashō's life, listing when the haiku master wrote which work and the significant events in Bashō's life.

Bashō himself wrote very little about the theory of haiku. We know a bit about Bashō's approach to haiku because of the writings of his disciples. His disciples would write things like, "And Bashō asked, 'What do you think of this haiku?' and the disciple would answer, 'I think this,' and Bashō would say, 'That is not right,' and then he would explain why."

Mr. Fukatsu explained to us that in Bashō's time there were many different schools of *renga*, or linked verse, existing side by side with the newer *hokku*, or haiku, form. Bashō was familiar with all the trends but did not feel comfortable with any of them. Eventually he struck out on his own, developing a unique style and approach in the course of his travels. Until Bashō, no one had traveled the way he had. His *Narrow Road to the Interior* was a milestone in the writing of haiku.

Bashō would go to different towns and hold poetry seminars at the home of local merchants. Usually he would write the first stanza while others, including local merchants, took turns writing the succeeding stanzas. In his *Narrow Road to the Interior*, Bashō included only the first stanzas. Separating that first stanza from the others is one of the many things that made Bashō unique.

Even more than Bashō, it was Mr. Fukatsu who intrigued me. What was it about Mr. Fukatsu that drew him to Bashō? I stayed after class one day, hoping to find the answer.

I was working as a manager in a nonferrous metal manufacturing company. Our head office was in Tokyo, and we had factories in northern Japan. In 1989, my company transferred me to Aizu Wakamatsu, an isolated rural town deep in Fukushima Prefecture. My wife and children had to stay behind, so that our kids could continue in the same schools. I don't think they do this in other countries, but here in Japan, it is not so unusual for workers and their families to be separated. It was really difficult for me. I was in my early fifties, with a wife and children, and suddenly I was living alone in a company dorm.

On top of being away from my family, for the first time in my life I was living in the countryside. I grew up in the city, in the busy shitamachi *section of Tokyo. Here I was in the midst of nature, surrounded by tall mountains and deep river gorges. In the winter, the snow was deep and white. The mountains were filled with cherry blossoms in the springtime.*

It was a twist of fate that landed me in Aizu Wakamatsu, but there I was. It would have been a waste to live in such a beautiful place and do nothing. I decided to start writing haiku. Before being transferred to Aizu Wakamatsu, I enjoyed reading haiku, but that's all. I was never the literary type. I studied economics in college, not literature.

Mr. Fukatsu connected with Momoko purely by chance. One day, in a used bookstore, he had picked up a copy of Momoko's first collection of haiku, *The Wooden Chair*. The book moved him deeply, and that is what made him decide to join her haiku group, Aoi.

Aizu Wakamatsu is four hours from Tokyo, so I made my visits back to my family coincide with Aoi haiku meetings.

I was starting to feel guilty about the amount of time I was spending away from my own family in pursuit of haiku, so I asked Mr. Fukatsu whether his family found it odd that, when he finally made it back home, he had developed a passion that did not include them. *Not at all,* he answered. *They were glad that I had developed an interest that made me feel less lonely in Aizu Wakamatsu. They were happy for me.*

That's how I started writing haiku. Just by chance. But once I started, it sort of took over my life. I lived in Aizu Wakamatsu for seven years. Time passed quickly. I was writing haiku, meeting many pleasant people. It was really a perfect haiku environment. I think my haiku went downhill after those seven years!

A few years after returning to Tokyo, Mr. Fukatsu retired. Momoko asked him to do some volunteer work and help manage her office. *So that's what I do every day now. I guess now that I think about it, my whole life really is steeped in the world of haiku.*

I asked Mr. Fukatsu why he especially liked Bashō. *I first liked his haiku because they are easy on the ear and easy to read. For many years, I didn't have any particularly deep knowledge of haiku, so I didn't understand Bashō's true value. But even reading him superficially, I could enjoy and admire his haiku. Bashō's haiku are beautiful to the novice and the expert alike.*

> 古池や蛙飛び込む水の音
> *furuike ya kawazu tobikomu mizu no oto*
>
> an old pond
> a frog hops in
> the sound of water

Everyone in Japan knows this haiku, whether they care for haiku or not. When I was a kid, I loved this haiku because I could picture the sound of the splash of water. As I studied more about haiku, I found it rich in other ways too. If you know a bit more about the era in which Bashō wrote it, for example, the poem becomes even more impressive. Mr. Fukatsu explained that in Bashō's day, a common phrase in traditional Japanese poetry was "the voice of the frog." *Just about any time you read a poem in those days about frogs it was "the voice of the frog." And then Bashō comes along, and his frog doesn't say a thing! It just jumps in the water and—plop!—the only sound is the splash. That is revolutionary. Imagine the reaction of people reading Bashō's haiku for the first time. It must have really stunned them.*

Mr. Fukatsu saw Bashō as always in pursuit of the fresh, the new, the revolutionary. At the same time, he felt Bashō was after eternal truth, goodness, and beauty. *These eternal qualities do not change, but what we define as beautiful changes with each generation. By experimenting with style and words, Bashō opened people's eyes to different kinds of beauty.*

Mr. Fukatsu recited several other well-known Bashō haiku:

さまざまの事思ひ出す桜かな
samazama no koto omoidasu sakura kana

oh so many things
recalled by
cherry blossoms

荒海や佐渡に横たふ天の河
araumi ya sado ni yokotau ama no kawa

the wild sea and
out toward Sado Island
the Milky Way[15]

閑かさや岩にしみいる蝉の声
shizukasa ya iwa ni shimiiru semi no koe

silence—
penetrating the rocks,
the cries of the cicada

Bashō wrote this last haiku on a visit to Risshakuji temple in Yamagata Prefecture. Mr. Fukatsu told me that one summer he went to see that same temple. *I sat in the quiet*, he said, *and thought about Bashō's haiku once again. I was wrapped in the same silence Bashō experienced when he heard the cries of the cicadas. I felt very close to Bashō at that moment.*

I told Mr. Fukatsu I had recently come across a stone lantern in a curiosity shop and was so taken with it that I bought it on the spot. The lantern was old and covered with moss. I paid for it, then hoisted it in pieces into the trunk of my car. Once home, I lugged it up to my apartment and set it on the balcony. Since then, I had been trying to write a haiku about my lantern, without any luck.

Oh, I know that feeling—of really wanting to write a haiku and not having it come out right at all. One of the first haiku I ever wrote was about a stone lantern. I was living in Aizu Wakamatsu.

蝶ひとつひぶくろにゐて夕立かな
chō hitotsu hibukuro ni ite yudachi kana

a single butterfly
taking shelter in the stone lantern—
summer downpour

I asked Mr. Fukatsu to show me other haiku he had
written. He rummaged around among his books until
he found an old copy of *Aoi* magazine and read out the
following:

末黒野にはや鳥のこゑあがりけり
sugurono ni haya tori no koe agarikeri

so soon from the scorched field
the cries of birds
rise up

*I was in Tochigi Prefecture at the time, a bit north of
Tokyo. It was early spring, a time when farmers are burning
the withered grasses in their fields. When I saw this field, it
had already been burnt. It was a deep black, and there was no
grass remaining. Yet I could hear birds already singing over
the field. Even though there was nothing left for them and no
sign of rebirth yet in the field, the birds were coming back. This
haiku came to me instantly, right on the spot. When a haiku
just comes to you like that, in the haiku world we call it a gift
sent from heaven.*

Mr. Fukatsu said it was rare for him to have a haiku

just spring to mind, fully formed. Although Momoko felt it was best to write a haiku on the spot, he often had to ponder an experience and play around with a haiku until he got it just right.

隠沼を呼びかはしつつ青葉木菟
komorinu o yobikawashitsutsu aobazuku

a turf-covered bog
the owls
hooting their love song

I was walking deep in the mountains of Sado Island one day in June, when I came across a turf-covered bog. There was no one around; silence reigned. Now and then, I would hear the hoot of two owls. They must have been facing each other across the swamp, as if one were singing a love song to the other. The silence and the scene made me recall the world of Zeami, a Noh writer and actor [1363–1443] in the Muromachi period. For reasons that are lost to history, the shogun sent Zeami into exile to Sado Island. It was indeed a world of silence and delicate beauty.

みんみんのみんなとほくになるゆふべ
minmin no minna tōku ni naru yūbe

the robust cries of the cicadas
and you far from me
in the evening

The first word of this haiku is minmin, *which is ono-matopoeic for a kind of cicada that chirps* miiinmiiin. *I wrote this haiku one day in August when I was visiting the botanical gardens in Tokyo. In the deep green of the gardens, robust cicadas were singing lustily. Despite their boisterous voices, I suddenly felt myself all alone, with the sense that others had left me behind. Now, at about that same time, my mother's illness took a turn for the worse, and shortly after that she was bedridden. Three months later she died, without seeing the New Year. I now think that this haiku, which came to me out of nowhere, was a foreboding of my mother's fate.*

Mr. Fukatsu began putting his papers and magazines away. I thanked him for all he had taught me that afternoon. He told me to keep my haiku simple. *Avoid a narrative or descriptive approach. If you are sad, don't write: "How sorrowful I am for the loss of my mother." Express it without using the words "sadness" or "joy." Haiku is a literature of silence.*

twelve

CHERRY BLOSSOMS

Having heard so much about cherry blossoms in Japan, I was determined to hate them. I didn't like how all the stores put up pink plastic flower decorations in mid-March, I didn't like living in a constant state of anticipation, and I didn't like picnics so crowded that I had to fight for space under a cherry tree. In fact, I never really cared for spring at all, with its expectations of lighthearted joy. Along with a minority of Japanese, I was drawn to February's plum blossoms, those hardy, dense, pink-and-white buds on dark, gnarled branches. Cherry blossoms last for only about a week, while plum blossoms cling tight for a good month.

The competition between admirers of plum and cherry blossoms reaches back hundreds of years. The most famous lover of plum blossoms was Sugawara no Michizane, a tragic ninth-century scholar, poet, and minister in the Heian imperial court. Although Sugawara no Michizane's brilliance earned him a high rank in the imperial adminis-

tration, it also provoked resentment in the powerful Fuji-
wara clan. To do away with him, the Fujiwaras convinced
a young new emperor that Sugawara no Michizane was
involved in a plot to overthrow the throne. Michizane was
banished to the remote island of Kyushu.[16] Before setting
off for exile, he composed this verse:

> When the east wind blows,
> Send me your perfume,
> Blossoms of the plum:
> Though your lord be absent,
> Forget not the Spring[17]

Michizane died in exile, a broken man. During his
years in Kyushu, he wrote some of Japan's most poignant,
well-known verse.

I was curious what Momoko had to say about Japan's
passion for cherry blossoms. Hoping to find solidarity with
her in the love of plum blossoms, I visited Momoko at her
cramped office in Tokyo's used-bookstore district.

The Aoi office was just off the busy road Yasukuni-
dōri, amid a row of old bookshops and mom-and-pop
stores. Momoko told me to look for the building with a
ramen shop on the ground floor, walk to the sushi take-
out window at the back, and take the elevator facing it up
to the seventh floor. Her office was the apartment with an
unfinished, homemade wooden door.

I rang the chime. *Hai, hai, coming, coming,* I could hear
Momoko moving inside. She opened the door and offered

me plastic slippers to wear inside. I took my coat off while Momoko phoned downstairs and ordered take-out sushi for us. The office consisted of one small, neat room packed with books. A worktable of blond wood dominated the center of the room. A kitchen sink and cutting board were tucked away in a recessed niche. The office had originally been a tiny studio apartment, but in recent years only businesses could afford to pay the exorbitant Tokyo rent.

As we waited for the sushi, we made small talk. Momoko is a fairly common girl's name in Japan, and I asked Momoko why she did not have a haiku name. *My own name seems to work just fine*, she answered. She told me that when she turned sixty, her friends suggested she should give herself a haiku name to mark the turning point. *But the number of brushstrokes used to write my name in Chinese characters is considered extra lucky, so I decided not to play with fate, and I kept the name I have.*

I told Momoko that I was not sure my haiku name was right for me. I explained how Dr. Mochizuki helped me choose it and Professor Kotani's reaction. Finally, with a bluntness only forgiven a non-Japanese, I asked Momoko if she would choose a new name for me. Momoko took my request in stride. *Not everyone has a haiku name. I don't, and neither does Professor Kotani. Her first name, Mizuhoko, is written with the Chinese characters for water and spear. It works well both as her real name and as a haiku name. But I will think of a haiku name for you, although it may take some time.*

The sushi deliveryman arrived and set out our meal of sushi, miso soup, and pickled vegetables on the large worktable. Momoko made us green tea and, with the scent of tea and sushi mingling in the air, turned to the matter of cherry trees.

She pulled from the shelf a heavy volume filled with pictures of ancient Japanese screens depicting cherry blossoms in the mountains, in valleys, and dipping gently over lakes. Kimono-clad women holding parasols sat in boats or on the grass beneath a tree. The screens exquisitely captured traditional Japanese ideals. Momoko pulled out a second book, this one of contemporary photographs of cherry trees, and began her private seminar. I was in a classroom of two—master and student, artist and observer.

The moon, the snow, cherry blossoms. One might say these are the three elements of beauty in Japan. Of these three, cherry blossoms reign supreme. The moon, though beautiful, appears every evening, and is less fleeting than cherry blossoms or snow. The snow is beautiful and evanescent, but unpredictable. Some winters the snow is plentiful, and at other times there is none. In some parts of Japan it snows almost year-round, while in other places it never snows. So there is less assurance of a common feeling evoked by snow in Japan.

There is a long tradition in Japan of respect and caring for cherry trees. For centuries, people here have admired cherry blossoms and tended their cherry trees, no matter how old or creaky the trees have grown. If you look at the photographs of cherry trees in this book, you will see that some of the trees are exactly the same trees that were depicted centuries ago in these ancient screens. We do not quite revere our cherry trees as gods. Not quite.

I wanted to understand the Japanese feeling for cherry trees. It occurred to me that if I had been learning haiku in America, I might have been exploring very different imagery. I could not think of a single common image that all Americans might be inspired to write about. There were famous and beautiful places, like the Grand Canyon or Niagara Falls, that surely were worthy of a haiku, but America was so large that many of us have never seen those places. I doubted that a flower existed that could be found in each of our fifty states. Perhaps this was why the English-language haiku that I read were so diverse, and seemed to emphasize images that were more directly self-expressive.

Every year, we wait as a nation for the cherry trees to bloom. In early March, like a child waiting for Christmas in the West, the cherry blossom season begins to pull at us, dominating our thoughts more and more each day. People make preparations for viewing cherry blossoms, sometimes with family, sometimes with friends, sometimes alone. In the old days, as in this screen, women wore special attire, a beautiful kimono, to view the cherry blossoms.

When I was very young, my mother used to take me to the forest hills to see the cherry trees. I remember thinking the flowers bloomed only for me. If we failed to make our annual pilgrimage, I was sure the trees would not be able to bloom!

When I was much older, yet still a young woman, I went back to making a pilgrimage to the cherry trees. I had graduated from college and was working at an advertising agency. I was so busy I stopped writing haiku. For some reason, just be-

fore turning thirty, I took stock of my life and decided I wanted to go through life as aware as possible of my humanity and my surroundings, so I set out to chronicle the passage of the seasons. I started writing haiku again, something I had fallen away from after college. It was at this point that I started visiting Japan's most famous cherry trees, going to a different spot each year. I call it my "encounter with spring." It took me twenty-seven years to complete this project. Each year, I would take leave from work to visit the trees.

Those were the "bubble" years in Japan. Everyone thought of only one thing: making money. People worked around the clock, and no one took time off. Imagine how odd it was, in that environment, for me to be requesting leave from my advertising company to go visit trees! Of course I did not tell people why I was taking these days off, but inside, I certainly felt different from the rest of society. That was quite stressful.

I recognized myself in Momoko's description of keeping quiet in the office about her poetic side. From time to time I had mentioned my interest in haiku to my Japanese colleagues, but I avoided talking about it with my American coworkers, sensing that they would consider me odd. Referring to an American politician who wrote poetry, a colleague at the office turned to me one day and said he couldn't figure out if the man was a poet who dabbled in politics or a politician who dabbled in poetry. I suppose I ought to have snapped back, *Maybe he did both well*, but instead I said nothing, and felt even more strongly that I needed to keep my haiku interest to myself.

Some years, I could not get away exactly at springtime.

But I managed to visit the trees nonetheless. I would go to wherever the trees happened to be in bloom. For example, sometimes I could only take leave in July, so I would go to Hokkaido, in the far north of Japan, where the cherry trees bloom very late. Or if I could get time off in January, I would go to Okinawa, Japan's southernmost island. So, in addition to encountering spring and the cherry trees, I ended up encountering my country.

I would go alone to see the trees. Some of the trees I visited had been alive for four or five hundred years. Yet a human life is shorter than a century. I would look at a tree for a while and start to think about the people who had come before me to look at it. I would sit before the blossoms for an hour, sometimes longer, and contemplate. I began to feel they were speaking to me.

花に問へ奥千本の花に問へ
hana ni toe okusenbon no hana ni toe

ask the cherry blossoms
of Okusenbon
ask the cherry blossoms

I wrote this one during one of my yearly pilgrimages. That year, I had gone to see the famous cherry trees of Okusenbon, on Mount Yoshino.

"Ask the cherry blossoms" is a line from a well-known Buddhist sermon given by Monk Ippen, who was a traveling monk. In this haiku, I liken my cherry-blossom pilgrimage to the pilgrimages of the Monk Ippen, and I evoke the addressing and questioning of one's self.

Momoko had been turning the pages in the book of photographs of cherry trees as she spoke. She stopped and asked me what the cherry blossoms I had seen that spring were like. *Were they new buds?* she asked. *Were they in full bloom? What time of day was it? How old were the trees?* I had to admit that all I could remember was that some blossoms were white and some were pink.

Momoko got up, went over to the shelf, and came back with a few large sheets of paper with printed columns of squares. *A whole set of words and phrases exist in Japan for describing cherry blossoms and cherry-blossom viewing. This is true for no other flower in Japan, not even the plum blossom.*

With a fat ink pen, she wrote the following, explaining each as she went along:

開花を待つ
kaika o matsu
waiting for blooming

初花
hatsuhana
the first blossom

花三分
hanasanbu
thirty percent blooming

一分咲き
ichibuzaki
blossoms at ten percent

満開
mankai
full bloom

花散る
hana chiru
blossoms falling

花過ぎて
hana sugite
blossoms are over

残花
zanka
lingering blossoms

朝桜
asazakura
morning cherry blossoms

夕桜
yūzakura
evening cherry blossoms

夜桜
yozakura
nighttime cherry blossoms

花かがり
hanakagari
cherry blossoms as seen by the light of a flame
or lamp under the tree

Each of these terms is used only for cherry trees, and contains a wealth of meaning. Asazakura *evokes a sense of freshness. It is the cherry blossom and the world without any pretense.* Yūzakura *implies a feeling of quiet, before the darkness of night has set in.* Yozakura *is fully night. It evokes a more luscious mood than "morning blossoms" might, for example.*

Hanakagari *refers to the custom of viewing cherry blossoms lit up at night. In olden days, candle lanterns were placed under the trees. In some parts of Japan, especially in Kyoto, candles are still used, but today it is generally more common to light the blossoms with electric lamps, usually placed on the ground, shining up toward the tree.*

I was born in Washington, D.C. and grew up in Maryland. As a child, I learned that Japan had donated the cherry trees lining the Tidal Basin of our nation's capital. My mother, from whom I inherited my adventurous spirit, would take us to see the cherry trees. When I was older, I took the bus downtown myself to see them. But in all those years, I had thought the cherry trees were only worth seeing when they were in full bloom. If we happened to go downtown before they were in full bloom, or after the blooms had peaked, I remember feeling we had somehow missed the event. It never occurred to me to find beauty or meaning in all phases of the cherry trees, or to seek to experience them at different times of the day.

What I had not considered until then was what Momoko called the almost sacred task of the haiku writer. By savoring each aspect of the cherry tree, by giving a name to its every mood, a haiku writer was breathing eternity into the fleeting blossoms, much as Biblical man did in naming the cattle, the fowl of the air, and the beast of the field.

さまざまの事思ひ出す桜かな
samazama no koto omoidasu sakura kana

oh so many things
recalled by
cherry blossoms
BASHŌ

From the time they are children, everyone in Japan participates in o-hanami, *cherry-blossom viewing. People will picnic under the cherry trees or go with their family to view the cherry blossoms. Over the years, we develop a bond with these trees. We grow up viewing cherry blossoms every year, discussing cherry blossoms, waiting for the cherry trees to bloom. Our lives are linked with the annual blossoming of the cherry trees.*

When we view the cherry blossoms, we are likely to recall previous visits to the cherry trees. It might have been with one's mother, who is now deceased. Or with a husband or wife who is no longer there. We see the blossom and we long for those we have loved.

みな過ぎて鈴の奥より花の声
mina sugite suzu no oku yori hana no koe

they have passed away
from deep in the bell
the voice of the cherry blossoms

KURODA MOMOKO

This is a haiku I wrote last year. Many people who have been so important to me are no longer alive. Last year, for example, I finished work on a two-volume set of interviews with thirteen of Japan's twentieth-century haiku writers. Some of these authors have since died. I have only their words in my heart to remind me of them. My mother is still alive, but she is very old, in her nineties. When she was younger, we used to talk for hours about haiku and about life. That part of her is gone, even though she is still alive. Bashō lives within me, but he is not alive either. The words of all of these people echo within me like the voice of the cherry blossoms, or like the bell we use at a temple or shrine to call the attention of the gods.

The sound of the bell and the voice of the cherry blossoms—they evoke feelings and memories and convey messages to me even without words.

I am in my sixties now. Many of the most important people who have shaped my life, including teachers, are dead. Yet they are not extinguished within me. When I see the cherry trees bloom, I recall them. My haiku is one of hope. It isn't a sad poem; it is full of beautiful memories.

thirteen

WITHERED FIELDS

I always wondered about the man at the Bunkyo University gathering who had written the haiku about his kidney operation.

> 腎臓に管うがたるる酷暑かな
> *jinzō ni kuda ugataruru kokusho kana*
>
> into my kidney
> a tube pierces
> ah, the summer heat!

I had only met him that one time, when I first embarked on my haiku journey. As I entered more deeply into the world of haiku, I would find myself thinking about the kidney haiku and the man who wrote it. He hadn't struck me as the haiku-writing type at the time, although by now I knew how diverse that universe really was. What inspired him to write such a haiku? Was it a special genre of haiku?

I found myself flipping through my *saijiki* to see if body parts were included as a sort of subset of seasonal words.

Now I wanted to meet him again. Traveling Man Tree had been at the Bunkyo University gathering too, so I started by calling him up. *Oh, Furuhata-san, the economics professor. I don't know him very well, but I can get you his address.*

Within the week, Traveling Man Tree had gotten back to me with his address, and I had written to Mr. Furuhata. After a silence of some days—in which I imagined Mr. Furuhata in hundreds of ways rejecting my request—the man wrote back that he would be happy to talk to me. He suggested we meet at the old Kinokuniya bookstore in the Shinjuku district of Tokyo, on the third floor, near the economic philosophy section.

We met on a Sunday afternoon. Shinjuku, in the heart of Tokyo, is probably one of the most crowded shopping areas on earth. On the day we met, the main street was closed off to cars and swarming with shoppers oblivious to the nation's economic downturn. There was a new Kinokuniya in the same neighborhood, all white marble and glass, but Mr. Furuhata preferred to meet in the old building, a narrow structure from the 1960s, with tinted windows and thick brown walls. It had been built at a time when Shinjuku was much less congested, and its two narrow elevators could now hardly meet demand. Crowds of people were standing in front of the elevators, and I gave up waiting, preferring to walk up the three flights to the economics section. There I found Mr. Furuhata, dressed in a pair of well-worn brown pants and a faded red polo shirt, flipping through a paperback. He was holding a black bag reminiscent of an old-fashioned doctor's case. He greeted me with a wave. *There's a coffee shop nearby that might be quieter*, he said and we walked back down, into the underground labyrinth of Shinjuku Station.

Like the bookstore, the coffee shop was also of another era, with tables and chairs made of thick wood in the colonial style and smoke filling the air. In the corner a young man on a break from work was slumped over, snoring away. The coffee shop reminded me of when I first came to Japan more than fifteen years earlier, before Starbucks squeezed tacky but interesting little shops like this one out of business. I was glad Mr. Furuhata had picked this place. We ordered some coffee and he began his tale.

Three years ago the doctors found cancer in my first kidney and removed it. So I was down to one kidney. It was hot, the middle of summer, and I was back in the hospital. I was in excruciating pain. I was lying on a bed and the nurse had turned me on my side, with my rear and my back exposed. This time they said it was kidney stones. But all I could think of was the cancer they found in my kidney the first time. The doctor said he was going to put a long tube in me, just below the kidney, and I was to wait until the kidney stone passed into the tube. The pain was awful.

It was just when the doctor stuck the tube into me—that's when I thought of my first haiku.

腎臓に管うがたるる酷暑かな
jinzō ni kuda ugataruru kokusho kana

into my kidney
a tube pierces
ah, the summer heat!

Can you believe it? I'm lying on the hospital bed, in hor-
rible pain, and suddenly I'm thinking of a seasonal word. My
pain is mingled with the heat. I'm outside myself, observing the
whole thing from an objective perspective. I had read a lot of
haiku before. I read the Nikkei *newspaper's haiku column every*
Sunday, but I never had the urge to write a haiku before this.

We spoke a little about reading haiku. He said he
liked the old stuff, Bashō and Shiki mostly. I asked him
what had made him go from reading haiku to actually
writing it.

For me it was a personal crisis. I had always liked read-
ing haiku, but it was only when I was going through a dif-
ficult time that I felt the need to write. You know, they say we
Japanese don't have a religion. Perhaps that's true. Buddhism
came to Japan over a thousand years ago but it isn't like Islam
or Christianity. For us, Buddhism is more a kind of philoso-
phy than a religion. It's part of our lives but it's not something
we're particularly conscious of. God is not the focus of its teach-
ing. So when I had a personal crisis, it didn't occur to me to
pray to God.

Mr. Furuhata's words reminded me of Sound of the
Tide, the historian in my haiku group, who told me she
started writing haiku because she needed something more

in her life. And I knew that some speculate that Bashō might never have become a great haiku master had he not been devastated, as a young man, by the loss of a companion from childhood. Issa, too, suffered more personal tragedies than seemed possible for one being. I wondered what drew me to haiku. Perhaps for some of us mortality itself is a crisis.

In Buddhism, everything changes; nothing stays the same. Cherry trees bloom, and then the petals fall off. Nations rise, then fall—Rome, England, perhaps America, perhaps Japan. Economies come and go. In one's own life, too, nothing stays the same. Change is happening all the time.

In Japan, everything is lush and green in the springtime, and cold and snowy in the wintertime. It's impossible not to be conscious of the seasons. So maybe the seasons speak to us more than any spiritual concept possibly could. In other countries where religion took root—Christianity, Islam—the land was dry, there was little green. The beauty of nature was less significant. But in Japan, the seasons have taken on great spiritual meaning.

So what do we do in the face of all of this? We try to capture and freeze an instant in time. A haiku is a snapshot of something that is moving and changing. It's not an eternity, but it's close enough. Maybe in Japan we write haiku instead of practicing religion because we have no God to turn to. And that's what I grasped at when I hit my spiritual crisis.

I asked Mr. Furuhata whether it was unusual to write a haiku when ill.

It's not unusual at all. We even have a name for it in Japan: it's called byōsho, *or illness writing. Shiki, who was ill for most of his life and died of tuberculosis when he was only thirty-five, wrote some great* byōsho.

Sickbed Snowfall
Four Poems by Shiki

(1)
It's snowing!
I can see it through the hole
in the *shōji* [18]

(2)
I keep asking
how deep
the snow's gotten

(3)
All I can think of
is lying here
in a house with all this snow

(4)
Open the *shōji*—
let me get a good look
at this Ueno snow! [19]

Mine are nowhere close to being as beautiful as Shiki's, so I am a little embarrassed to show you my poetry, but here is another illness haiku I wrote:

四年たち転移もなくて蕗の薹

yonen tachi ten'i mo nakute fuki no tō

four years now
no sign of spread—
the butterbur stalk

This haiku also is about my cancer. When you have cancer and it's been removed, they tell you that if it doesn't come back in five years, then you're safe. I wrote this poem in the fourth year after my kidney was removed. It's springtime, and I'm almost out of the woods. There's a sense of hope and expectation. Maybe it's okay to dream of the future again, to look ahead. For the first time in a long time, I am not afraid to notice the butterbur stalk growing and coming to life again. Two separate things—the butterbur flower and cancer—have become connected. The butterbur has somehow become a sign of hope for me.

Mr. Furuhata's discussion of sickness haiku taught me that haiku did not always have to be about happy emotions. A haiku could be about anything, really. A while back, someone had told me about erotic haiku. At the time, I was skeptical and thought that perhaps this kind of writing was not "real" haiku. Now I was convinced I had been wrong. Haiku could easily encompass themes of sickness, erotica, death, and it did not have to be limited to the so-called "noble" emotions, but it could include all of those lesser but very common negative feelings like fear, doubt, suspicion, jealousy.

I asked Mr. Furuhata if he thought that it was necessary to have had a spiritual crisis to write good haiku. He took his time answering, sipped his coffee, and contemplated the young man asleep at the next table over.

Well, some people write haiku about their travels or their day-to-day experiences. But to write a really deep haiku, I think the poem has to address life itself. Otherwise it's kind of thin.

He took his doctor's-bag-like briefcase from the empty chair beside him, set it on the table, and started pulling out papers, looking for something.

There are other spiritual crises a human being goes through in the course of life. Maybe crisis is too strong a word. How about turning point? In Japan, reaching the age of seventy is a turning point in life. It's customary to write poems at around that time. On my seventieth birthday, I sent about a dozen poems I had composed to my friends, along with an invitation to my birthday celebration. I've got them here, somewhere.

It was at the age of seventy that Dr. Mochizuki, the head of our haiku group, began writing haiku. There was something poignant about the thought that people all over Japan were marking their seventieth birthdays with poetry.

Ah, here they are! Mr. Furuhata picked out a few of the ten he had composed for his seventieth birthday and read them out to me.

若き日に想いし人の賀状かな
wakaki hi ni omoishi hito no gajō kana

oh! youthful days
from a long-lost sweetheart—
a New Year's greeting

This is a poem about a long-lost love. It's the feeling you have when you receive a New Year's card from someone you haven't seen or heard from for maybe thirty, forty years. It's someone for whom maybe you had a hidden love when you were young, when you were eighteen or so, and you have never told a soul. And now, here you are, an older person, your life has been long, you've traveled many roads. You get the mail, sit down to read it, and out falls this card from someone who meant so much to you decades ago. And you've never told anyone about it. Yes, that's what I was feeling.

雪に降る雨の音きく初湯かな
yuki ni furu ame no oto kiku hatsuyu kana

hearing the sound of rain
falling on snow
first bath of the year

See, this one is okay, but it isn't very deep. I'm watching the snow while getting ready for my bath, hearing the sound of running water, like rain. It's rather pretty, though.

地下鉄を出れば雪舞う古書の街
chikatetsu o dereba yuki mau kosho no machi

leaving the subway
snow dancing
old books district

This one has nice images, but it's not particularly profound.
I like going to the secondhand bookstore neighborhood in Tokyo,
so this haiku reminds me of that.

We ordered more coffee. The young man sleeping in
the back of the shop had stopped snoring and seemed to
be sleeping more peacefully now. As the afternoon wore
on, others too had come in off the busy street for a nap.
This coffee shop, with its dim lighting, seemed to be a
magnet for all the tired businessmen in the area.

In the West, right before you die, what do you do? You
pray to God. You get closer to your religion maybe. Well, in
Japan, do you know what many of us do? We try to write a
final poem that will sum up our life. A tanka [five-seven-
five-seven-seven syllable form] *or a haiku, the form doesn't*
matter, but we try to reduce our life to one essential poem that
sums it all up. When I die, I want people to say, "Ah, he wrote
a beautiful final haiku."

I had read Bashō's death poem:

旅に病んで夢は枯野をかけ廻る
tabi ni yande yume wa kareno o kakemeguru

ill on a journey
my dreams through withered fields wander
BASHŌ

The tradition didn't end with Bashō, though. Just recently, there was a famous essayist who passed away, Ekuni Shigeru. He had cancer for many months before he died. Every day he wrote a haiku. This is his final haiku:

おい癌め酌みかはさうぜ秋の酒
oi ganme kumikawasau ze aki no sake

hey, you cancer!
together let's down a round
of fall sake
EKUNI SHIGERU (1934–97)

Toward the end of his days, cancer became his companion. Just as before he might have been out until late with his drinking buddies; now he was drinking sake—just him and his cancer.

I asked Mr. Furuhata if he expected to write a final haiku.

Of course, I'm working on one now. It would be sad to die without having one ready. But it's hard for me to write haiku without a feeling of crisis. Maybe I should join a haiku group, but I really like to write alone.

❊   ❊   ❊

Some months after our meeting in the coffee shop I called Mr. Furuhata to follow up on our conversation about haiku. He came on the line, and I offered the usual Japanese greeting. *O-genki desu ka? Are you healthy?*

Not so well, I'm afraid. I just got out of the hospital last week. Suffered a heart attack. It was completely unexpected. I was rushed to the hospital in an ambulance. But I'm fine now. It's nothing to worry about. They say I'll be back to normal in a month or so.

I told him I was sorry to hear about his heart attack. And then I couldn't resist. *Tell me, did you write any haiku after your heart attack?*

You bet! They had me strapped down in the ambulance and it just popped into my head on the way to the hospital!

鳥雲にわれ括られて救急車
torikumo ni ware kukurarete kyūkyūsha

a flock of birds dense as a cloud
and me all bound up
in an ambulance

3

調和

chōwa

HARMONY

fourteen

CHILDREN'S DAY

I bicycled through the streets of Tokyo under a bright blue sky, fresh from a visit to my calligraphy teacher. She had given me the good news that I had moved up a rank in calligraphy. I was still in the beginner ranks, but no longer at the very bottom. I wished for a ranking system in haiku, so that I could have my progress validated, but this seemed to run counter to the whole concept of haiku as a personal exploration.

It was May 4, the day before Children's Day, and on my way out, my calligraphy teacher had given me some sprigs of *shōbu*, the reedy stem of the iris flower, saying, *It's for your son, for Boys' Day*, using the prewar term for Children's Day. *Put the* shōbu *in his bathwater. It has a delicious scent, and it cures tiredness in little boys.* She showed me with her hands how children like to make a whistle by pulling the *shōbu* reed taut between their thumbs, and blowing. I had never heard of putting *shōbu* in bathwater for Children's Day, but I bowed and thanked her for the gift.

I parked my bike in the garage, took the plastic bag with the *shōbu* leaves off the handlebar, and took the elevator up to my apartment. Once inside, I put the leaves in the refrigerator and promptly forgot about them.

The next day, Children's Day, was exceptionally beautiful. Like many Japanese families, we celebrated the holiday outdoors, in our case with a hike through the woods of Kamakura, about an hour south of Tokyo. My children helped pack sandwiches, and I threw into the backpack a collection of haiku by members of Aoi for inspiration.

The train out of Tokyo was filled with like-minded enthusiasts, and we got off by the hundreds at North Kamakura Station, each of us pretending we were alone communing with nature. To get to the hiking paths, we cut through Kenchōji temple, Japan's oldest Zen training monastery. As we walked through the temple, I took the Aoi collection out of my backpack and read.

牡丹を御佛として数えけり
bōtan o mihotoke toshite kazoekeri

peonies
like Buddhas
I count them

KAZUMA ASAJI, AOI MEMBER

うぐひすの声もいつしか午後なりし
uguisu no koe mo itsushika gogo narishi

the warbler's
cry and unnoticed
comes the afternoon
SAITŌ MASAYA, AOI MEMBER

Our hike took us through gorgeous hills and valleys.
A mountain stream cut across our path. We stopped and
listened to the stream until there was nothing in our minds
but the sound it made, and then we hopped from rock to
rock, to reach the other side. We picnicked in a clearing,
brushing the bugs off our food. I toyed with a haiku in my
mind:

かめむしと黄色たくあん子供の日
kamemushi to kiiro takuan kodomo no hi

stinkbugs
and pickled yellow radish
—Children's Day

We emerged from the forest sometime in the late
afternoon and walked through farmland, past summer
cottages, until we reached Kamakura's Great Buddha,
a bronze statue of Amida Buddha almost forty feet tall.
There we sat and rested from our long hike. I recalled a
haiku by Shiki:

大佛のうつらうつらと春日かな
daibutsu no utsurautsura to harubi kana

the Great Buddha
dozing
on a spring day
SHIKI

It was early evening when we got back to Tokyo. My feet ached, and it was then that I remembered the *shōbu* reeds. I filled the tub and threw in a sprig, saving the rest for my son.

I wallowed in the tub, wondering whether there was any scientific basis to the reputed soothing quality of the *shōbu* leaves. I checked my watch on the sink. Four minutes had gone by. I didn't think the *shōbu* leaves were working. They were supposed to give off a delicate scent, but I couldn't smell a thing.

I thought about the haiku I had written on our picnic that day. I was fine at images but not good at all at infusing them with meaning. What was I trying to say?

Was there a hidden key I was missing and needed to find? What should I be looking for?

With my toe I turned on the hot water faucet. I slid further down into the tub until my head was completely covered. From below, I made bubbles and watched them break to the surface. My listless arms floated to the top like two pieces of cedar. I counted to see how long I could stay under water. I slid back up to a sitting position and watched the waterline drop.

I was learning, through haiku, to look at the world differently. And I was learning this from a society notorious for stifling the individual. Despite the emphasis on controlling the group (or perhaps because of this), millions of Japanese were writing poetry, the most individualistic of arts, as part of the natural flow of their lives.

I would meet haiku amateurs in the most unlikely places. One afternoon while riding on the Ginza Line, I struck up a conversation with the man sitting next to me, a slightly balding businessman dressed in a traditional ink-blue suit. He said that he worked as a manager for a construction company, but that his real passion was haiku. He opened his briefcase to show me, and out spilled several haiku magazines and a notebook with his most recent verses.

Perhaps all these people had discovered something I was just now learning: that survival in an increasingly complex world requires each of us to tend to our souls, our individuality, more than ever. I needed to nurture my ability to see the world as I saw it, not as others might see it.

Outside the bathroom I could hear my son Sam coming up the steps. I let the water out of the tub and dried myself off. He knocked on the door, asking if it was his turn yet to take a bath. I wrapped myself in a towel and opened the door. He stood naked, eagerly awaiting his turn, *shōbu* in hand. I filled the tub once again and he climbed in, squatted, enjoying the feel of the water splashing his toes.

He took the *shōbu* and gently drew it through the water as it rose. Soon he was sitting with water up to his waist. Completely absorbed by the novelty of having a leafy plant in his tub, he brought the *shōbu* close to his face, smelled it, and then split it in two, releasing its scent. He tore off a piece from the top and put it between his thumbs, then brought it to his mouth, trying to coax a whistle out of the leaves, just as my calligraphy teacher had said he would. I turned the faucet off and watched him play. After a few minutes he looked at me and said, *These plants really work. I can feel it! My tiredness is all gone.*

黄あやめの水にのりだす子供かな
kiayame no mizu ni noridasu kodomo kana

into the *shōbu* water
ventures the child

NATORI SATOMI, AOI MEMBER

THE O-BON FESTIVAL

It was August 15, the first day of the *o-bon* festival, when the spirits of the dead are said to return to earth. In keeping with tradition, many of my friends had returned to their hometowns to visit the graves of their ancestors.

いくたりか生者と遭ひぬ墓参り
ikutarika shōja to ainu hakamairi

meeting
lots of living souls
upon my visit to the graveyard
UEDA GOSENGOKU (1933–97)

I marveled at the idea that most Japanese knew where their ancestors were buried. My ancestors had lived and died all over the world. Their remains were in graveyards in America, Chile, France, England, Israel, Moldova, Russia, and Poland. Further back, and I might also include

Spain. My Chilean grandmother's ashes were sprinkled over Bodega Bay, California. There were also those who never had the dignity of a grave. That, too, was part of my history.

One of the hardest things about being a diplomat was that I lived so much of my life away from my extended family. When I was overseas, I was able more or less to maintain the illusion that my parents were not aging, and that time was frozen. It was only on trips back to America that I was forcibly struck with the passage of time. I had missed marriages, births, illnesses, and death.

The streets of Tokyo were empty. The hot, humid air of the city made those of us who stayed feel heavy and sluggish. In the daytime, the cicadas sang a deafening tune.

窓閉めて七階の部屋蝉時雨
mado shimete nanakai no heya semishigure

window closed
up to the seventh floor
cascading cries of the cicada

PUNGENT GRASS, DELICATE WATER

At night the cockroaches took over the streets. I was finding summer a good season for haiku writing.

I called my calligraphy teacher to see if we would be having a lesson. She said she did not expect her other students to come by, but she invited me over anyway. When I arrived, she set out the familiar bottle of ink, slate dish, and stack of brown rice-paper. I kneeled down to work, apologizing for coming to see her during the *o-bon* festival. *It's no bother at all. I'm from Tokyo, so I don't observe the festival in August anyway. I visit my ancestors' graves in July.*

I had never heard of people celebrating *o-bon* in July, and asked her what she meant. She explained that in the late-nineteenth-century Meiji era, after Japan had opened up to the West, the emperor issued a decree ordering everyone to stop using the lunar calendar. It was part of the government's plan to modernize Japan by adopting Western standards. All of Japan's holidays moved up a month, to conform to the Western, solar calendar. The New Year, which had always been celebrated in early February, was now celebrated on January first. *O-bon*, which until then had been celebrated in mid-August, moved up to mid-July.

Tokyoites went along with this because we were eager for modernity, but people in the countryside refused to switch over. O-bon *involves honoring the dead, and on top of that, the country folk are farmers, and the rhythm of the harvest is everything to them. Eventually, the farmers won out, and Tokyo merchants, many of whom employed people from the countryside who insisted on going back home for the holiday in August, gave up and went back to observing* o-bon *on August 15.*

Sugiyama-sensei concluded that her father had been a merchant in Nihonbashi, in the west of the city. Her family's Tokyo roots went back three hundred years. All of her ancestors were buried in Tokyo, and she still liked to celebrate *o-bon* in July. *That's what a real Tokyoite should do.* She spoke of the Meiji-era changes as if they had happened only a few years ago, in her lifetime.

As my teacher predicted, no other students came to class that evening. We were alone, enjoying the chat. Sugiyama-sensei went upstairs and came back down with two cups of green tea on a lacquer tray.

By now, my teacher was familiar with my haiku interest, and it did not take long for our conversation to turn to that subject. I asked if the change in calendar explained why some haiku seasonal words seem oddly out of season. I had always been puzzled that a common haiku term for the New Year was "first spring."

初春の終点ちかき駅に降り
hatsuharu no shūten chikaki eki ni ori

first spring
getting off the train
near the end of the line

HIRAI SHŌBIN (1931–2003)

Sugiyama-sensei concurred. *Yes, that's the problem. Under the old calendar, New Year's Day came sometime in early February, just as the plum blossoms appear. That is why many of the older haiku about the New Year use terms like "spring is coming," or "first spring." Today, it seems odd to write a haiku about "first spring" on January 1, but 150 years ago, when the New Year was in February, it made perfect sense.*

Even after the emperor's edict, many haiku poets stuck to the old calendar in their writing. Shiki, who lived during the Meiji period, seems to have ignored the edict completely:

梅提げて新年の御慶申しけり
ume sagete shinnen no gyokei mōshikeri

bearing plum blossoms
speaking New Year's greetings
SHIKI

That evening I worked on a page of calligraphy by Ōgishi, the fourth-century Chinese calligrapher. Many of the characters were no longer in use in Japan, victims of postwar Ministry of Education reforms. As I copied the characters, Sugiyama-sensei sighed, *It isn't just during the Meiji era that the government imposed reforms. After the war, the Americans came in and were full of ideas for change.* She explained that during the Occupation the Ministry of Education simplified the writing system, bringing the number of Chinese characters in use in Japan down from about ten thousand to less than two thousand. She was still angry about the changes imposed nearly half a century ago. *The Ministry of Education did an especially poor job of it. Not only did they do away with the richness of our writing, but they were very sloppy in the way they simplified the characters. No wonder children today are confused!*

I once met an elderly man in northern Japan who belonged to a haiku group that rejected the postwar simplification of the writing system. Members of that group wrote haiku drawing on over ten thousand Chinese characters formerly in use in Japan, not just the two thousand that survived the postwar reforms.

I told my calligraphy teacher about this man's haiku

group, and she nodded her approval. *Just think of the haiku by Bashō or Issa or even Shiki, written with characters no longer in use today. Haiku is a visual art too. It is a pity we have sacrificed some of the beauty of our poetry.*

The Numamomo haiku group would be meeting on the last day of the month, and I told Sugiyama-sensei I was having trouble coming up with five haiku. I explained that I had bought an old Japanese stone lantern some time back, and that since then I had been trying to write a haiku about it.

> 草高き石灯籠や...
> *kusa takaki ishidōrō ya . . .*
>
> the tall summer grasses
> a stone lantern and . . .

But I couldn't quite decide how to end it. I asked Sugiyama-sensei what she thought of my ending it with *atsusa kana,* or "Ah! The heat."

Heibon! Too common! She replied. *It sounds as if you borrowed the word from someone else's haiku.*

What if I end it with semi no koe, *or the voice of the cicadas?*

Heibon! Too common! It isn't coming from your heart.

What about shizuka kana, *or "Ah! The quiet?"*

Heibon, heibon, heibon! You are mixing contemporary haiku with language straight from Bashō. She dismissed them all.

I knew that Sugiyama-sensei was right and that my

knowledge of Japanese was too imperfect. Sometimes this led me to produce unusual haiku, winning praise from other members of the Numamomo haiku group, but more often it just made my haiku clunky.

Seeing my disheartened look, my teacher proposed:

草高き石灯籠や星流れ
kusa takaki ishidōrō ya hoshinagare

tall grasses
a stone lantern
shooting stars

Then she shook her head, *This haiku is not very good. I've mixed too many images. Also, I am not sure why you are writing about the grasses when your lantern is on your balcony.*

I told her it was just fine. I had four other haiku at home, so now I was set. In a flush of gratitude, I asked Sugiyama-sensei to come along with me to Numazu for the next session of my haiku group. She thought about it for a moment and then declined, saying calligraphy kept her busy enough. *Besides, I haven't written haiku in years, and I have no talent for it.*

sixteen

THE VILLAGE LEADER

The phone rang. It was Sugiyama-sensei on the line. She had been thinking about my invitation to come to Numazu for the haiku class. Perhaps she had been too hasty in her decision. Her husband's family was from Shizuoka Prefecture, near Numazu, and she used to go there frequently before he died. She had not been in years. Perhaps she would join me after all.

The following weekend we took the early morning train out of Tokyo. I wanted to surprise my haiku group by wearing a *yukata*, a colorful, long Japanese cotton robe often worn in the summertime. My calligraphy teacher showed up in a dress she told me she bought from a merchant at the foot of the pyramids in Egypt. Like a young child who cannot picture her second-grade teacher having an existence outside of the classroom, I could not imagine my calligraphy teacher in Egypt, or, for that matter, anywhere other than in her makeshift classroom, doing calligraphy.

198

The train came into the station, and I followed Sugi-
yama-sensei into the car. *Let's sit on the right side, where we
can see Mount Fuji*, she said, hurrying to find good seats
for us. We were not disappointed. A little while into the
ride, Mount Fuji's familiar lopsided silhouette came into
view. On one side the mountain made a sharp, purposeful
climb up from the earth. On the other it meandered down,
unburdened by its reputation, tapering off somewhere in
the rich fields below.

I once spent an entire afternoon searching in my
library for haiku about Mount Fuji. Finding only a few, I
had asked Momoko why this was so. *Perhaps the image is
too big and imposing*, she replied. *If you write a haiku about
Mount Fuji, everyone has a picture in mind of the mountain.
It is difficult to get away from that image. There is no room left
for silence and subtlety.*

Sugiyama-sensei and I spent the train ride discuss-
ing each other's haiku. Not having had the time to write
five haiku in advance, she had brought along an old note-
book of hers from a time many years ago when she wrote
haiku. She debated which five to choose. *It's August, so you
should pick haiku with summer seasonal words*, I suggested
presumptuously.

After a stretch of silence, Sugiyama-sensei turned
to me and asked what it was that attracted me to haiku.
Her question startled me. I was so used to asking other
people about haiku that I had never really sat down and
consciously considered my own reasons for enjoying haiku.
When I first asked Traveling Man Tree this same question,

he had answered *I do haiku* and differentiated it from golf, which for him was simply a hobby.

I searched for an answer. *It's like a kiss. No one works at producing a good kiss. It just happens.*

She must think I am crazy, I thought to myself. I tried a different tack.

In my work, I deal with matters that are so large that the individual can sometimes seem insignificant. Yet composing a haiku demands that I respect my individuality. Momoko once told me to write a haiku that is like me, not like Bashō. I think that writing haiku brings balance into my life.

Sugiyama-sensei nodded her understanding. *Do you know why I decided to come to Numazu with you? It was my husband. His voice called to me from the heavens.* She raised her thin arm up high, pointing her palm upward and bringing it slowly to her heart, to make sure I understood what she was saying. *He said to me, "You should visit Shizuoka Prefecture, my childhood home." So I thought to myself, "How could I not find the time to go to Numazu to honor my dead husband?" That's why I am here on this train with you today.*

We were late getting to the Goyōtei, and by the time we arrived, everyone was seated and writing out their haiku. I stepped onto the tatami mat in my *yukata,* and from the class came a collective intake of breath and then applause as the group took in my classic Japanese summer dress. I bowed, grinned, and took my place at one of the low tables. Sugiyama-sensei sat beside me, and I explained to her what to do with each piece of paper. Out of the corner of my eye, I could see Momoko watching me with approval.

That day, only one person chose one of my haiku:

足指をくすぐる草の盆祭り
ashiyubi o kusuguru kusa no bon matsuri

grass tickling
my toes
o-bon festival

No one chose my stone lantern haiku. At the end of the session, when Momoko asked if anyone had anything to add, I raised my hand. *A few months ago, I bought a stone lantern. Since then I've worked hard to write a good haiku about it. Even though I finally came up with one, no one selected it. Instead, a haiku that I wrote very quickly, without nearly as much thought, was chosen. How should I interpret this?*

Momoko looked at me with surprise: *Why would you expect your first haiku about your stone lantern to succeed? You must write and write and write. After you write a hundred haiku about your lantern, maybe then a good one will emerge. In the meantime, you must keep writing. There is no room for impatience in haiku.*

Some time back, Dr. Mochizuki had decided that each of our haiku sessions should end with a banquet. So, our haiku session over, we piled into cars and drove to a nineteenth-century Japanese inn about ten minutes away from the Goyōtei, set back from the road and surrounded by pine trees. Two middle-aged women in kimono greeted us at the entrance. Carp swam lazily in a pond off to the side. A stone lantern stood, slightly tilted, at the edge of the pond. I looked at it. *Keep writing*, it seemed to be whispering to me.

Dr. Mochizuki was the major-domo at our banquets, while Momoko sat at the place of honor. That evening's seasonal cooking included sashimi, braised eggplants, and delicate summer vegetables flavored with woodsy herbs. From the trunk of his car Dr. Mochizuki brought in a case of an exclusive brand of sake. As he placed a bottle at each table, he explained to me, *This brand comes in seven different grades, with seven the lowest, and one the best. Tonight we are having grade four sake, which is so good that you will feel joy in life the moment it touches your lips. As for grades three and higher,* he said with a twinkle in his eye, *you must discover those for yourself.*

The conversation flowed with the sake. Dr. Mochizuki spoke first that night:

This month is the third anniversary of the Numamomo haiku group. I was seventy years old when I started the group. If you had told me, when I was thirty, that in forty years I would be launching a haiku group, I would not have believed you. I was far too busy trying to achieve success in my medical profession.

Thirty years ago I started my own hospital. I was anxious. I felt that I was taking a big risk. It was a huge commitment. I thought, "Maybe I will do this until I am fifty-five or sixty at the most." When I turned sixty, I couldn't believe I was still running my own hospital. I thought, "Well, I don't feel so old. Maybe I'll be able to do this for another five years." So I kept going. Now I am over seventy, toasting you here tonight, still running my own hospital. Inside, I am thinking to myself, "I wonder how many more years I have left? One? Maybe two?" I don't know. But I don't feel ready to quit, and I am grateful for every day of my life.

It was Momoko's turn to talk. She told us a story of a trip she recently had made to the isolated mountain village of Okuaizu, near the Tadamigawa Dam. The dam was one of many built after the war when Japan was growing fast and needed more electricity. There were nine small villages near the dam, some of which had a population of no more than a few hundred.

In one of the smallest villages near Okuaizu lives a man named Baba-san. He is ninety-three years old, and he has been writing haiku since about the age of thirteen. He wrote to ask me to lead a haiku convention he was organizing for his town and the surrounding villages. I agreed, and along with three other haiku experts, we traveled to Okuaizu to be the selectors for Baba-san's haiku convention.

When Baba-san was young, the mountain villages had no schools beyond the elementary grades. But he could not leave his mountain village to study because his father was the village leader and he was the eldest son. Baba-san would inherit the role of village leader, and he had many things to learn from his father. So Baba-san studied in the little schoolhouse up to the sixth grade, and he tried to continue for another two years there, but had to quit. Baba-san has been writing haiku since the age of thirteen, even though he has only an eighth-grade education.

Momoko explained that Baba-san's father was an *izan-san*, or learned man. Before the war, villages—particularly in rural areas—usually had one person who would stand out as a man of learning, most likely in the Chinese classics or Chinese poetry. Such a person earned the name *izan-san. Baba-san was always greatly respectful and proud of his father, and so he took the name Izanshi, or "son of a learned man" as his haiku name.*

Even when Baba-san was young, he had to work hard, always seeking new ways for his village to survive economically. When the war came it was especially difficult to be the village leader. Baba-san had to figure out how to keep everyone from going hungry. They had to give the government all the metal equipment they had used for farming, to melt it down for weapons. It was very tough for his village. After the war, Baba-san figured there would be a need for textiles, and so he decided his whole village should go into the business of shepherding and spinning wool, since this did not require a lot of metal equipment. This worked for a while, but then synthetics came into fashion and his village couldn't compete with the big textile manufacturers. So Baba-san shifted his whole village to beekeeping.

Even though Baba-san was unable to continue with school and devoted his life to his village, he never stopped writing haiku. He has been writing haiku for eighty years!

Today Baba-san and his wife, a spry young woman of eighty-nine, like to hike in the woods and marshes near their home, writing haiku along the way. When Baba-san hikes, he puts his things in a furoshiki, *a cotton cloth, the old-fashioned way, tying a knot and carrying it on his back. While we might turn to our electronic pocket dictionaries to look up an unusual reading for a particular Chinese character, Baba-san checks his words in a huge hardback copy of the Kōjien dictionary. That dictionary probably weighs about three kilos! Baba-san just loads the Kōjien up in his* furoshiki *and lugs it with him through the woods. He will stop from time to time to set his cotton cloth on a rock, untie it, and search through his dictionary. In some ways, he is completely oblivious to changing times.*

Baba-san's wife is named Shikitai. That is an elegant, classical Japanese name. Shikitai's parents, themselves born in a mountain village in nineteenth-century Japan, somehow chose such a name for their daughter. Just think of Baba-san and Shikitai, an elderly couple with almost no formal education, living in an isolated mountain village, writing haiku.

Baba-san still thinks like the village leader he was raised to be. When I met him, he showed me the seasonal word index he is writing for his mountain village. He is almost a century old, and yet he is undaunted, embarking on something new.

Momoko knew that I would soon be leaving Japan. I had told her earlier that day that I was worried my connection with Japanese haiku would fade once I left. I did not think I would be able to keep writing haiku, or to keep growing in ways haiku had taught me. I felt a door was about to close, and time was running out. Now she turned and faced me directly.

How can you worry about the future, when you will be a

different person when the time comes? Besides, what you think and feel now is different from what you thought and felt when you were twenty, or when you were thirty. When you leave Japan, you will think and feel different things. New doors will open.

You can write haiku wherever you are. There is no reason to stop. Think of Baba-san. He is ninety-three years old, and he is still writing haiku, and still coming up with new dreams and plans.

Momoko turned back to the entire group and said, *There are extraordinary people like Baba-san and Shikitai all over Japan, all over the world—people you never read about or hear about. Everywhere there are people living remarkable lives. These are the people who guide us in life.*

I had always loved adventure and meeting new people, but had viewed such pursuits as mere pastimes. That night, I was gaining insight into my life from Momoko and from a ninety-three-year-old man from the Japanese countryside—a man whom I had never met and who, in turn, knew nothing of me. I recalled something Traveling Man Tree had said when I first met him. He explained how devoting himself to haiku had led him to change the way he approached life—now he took all the small corners of the world that presented themselves to him on their own terms. I was finally beginning to see what he meant.

seventeen

A NAME

My three-year tour in Japan was coming to a close. The shipping company had loaded our life into four wooden crates. I lay on the grass watching the moving crew seal each crate and hoist it into the container that was to be shipped to America. The clouds above moved swiftly. I watched as a swirl of white pulled away from one large cloud, and joined other swirls. The wind swept this new cloud across the sky, and another cloud appeared from behind a Tokyo high-rise.

My family had survived my haiku adventure. As a working mother, I had thought that adding a hobby to my life would be irresponsible and selfish. A voice inside me always seemed to tell me that any extra time I might carve out in my day ought to go to more time with my husband and children. (Ironically, that voice had not come from my husband and children.) Now I saw that finding something that gave me personal pleasure and that kept me growing as a human being made me a much more pleasant person to be around. My children needed me, but they were getting older and our relationship was changing. My developing an interest beyond my family gave my children the space they needed to grow too.

My career also seemed to have survived my passion for haiku. I was cautious about revealing my haiku self to my colleagues at work because I thought they would consider it a weakness or a distraction from my diplomatic duties. Over time I saw that the real problem was not how they might react, but my own self-doubt. The more I became invested in haiku, the more confident I was about it. Now when I told people about my interest in haiku, I hardly noticed their reaction, positive or negative.

Although I regretted leaving Japan, I was looking forward to my next assignment, back in Washington. It would be nice to be closer to my parents. My father would soon turn eighty-two. Time weighed. When I was a teenager, my father and I would have long, sometimes tense, conversations about politics and war, about the atomic bomb and the Manhattan Project. Now I had different questions about life. My father had worked on the Manhattan Project when he was drafted into the army. I was curious about the work he had done after the war. Had he made a conscious choice to work on nuclear non-proliferation, or was this simply how his life had evolved? Did my life have an overarching meaning that I needed to glean before moving forward? Would meaning be revealed only in retrospect? Or perhaps I was approaching the problem the wrong way. Perhaps, as in haiku, meaning would appear only in flashes.

❀   ❀   ❀

There was one last thing I needed to do before leaving Japan. Some months back, Momoko had promised she would choose a haiku name for me. I had not heard from her since. The Numamomo haiku group was meeting the week before my departure, and I resolved to attend, knowing this would be my last chance to ask her about my name.

That day's haiku session took place, as the sessions had from the beginning, in a spirit of warmth and friendliness. We were thirty at this, my last meeting, about the same number as when I first nervously left my shoes at the door to enter the Goyōtei. Now I saw that we had all come to haiku from very different life experiences, but that we were bound together by our dedication to this art. Professor Kotani's husband had died two weeks earlier, after an arduous twenty-year struggle with illness, but she had come to see me off despite her personal sorrow. When several people selected her haiku, she boomed out her name, proud of her progress:

> 飛翔する光の中をほととぎす
> *hishō suru hikari no naka o hototogisu*

soaring
in the bright light
—the cuckoo

Momoko read out a farewell haiku she had composed
for me:

皐月富士別るるは又逢はむため
satsuki fuji wakaruru wa mata awamu tame

Mount Fuji in June
leaving so as once again
to meet

Momoko announced that she had one more task to
complete before I left the country.

*Several weeks ago, Abigail-san came to me and asked
whether I might choose a new haiku name for her. Dr. Mochi-
zuki had helped her choose the one she now has—Pungent
Grass, Delicate Water—but she told me that many people have
said it is an odd haiku name and that she herself is unsure it
suits her.*

Momoko looked over at Dr. Mochizuki and added
playfully, *Don't you know, Dr. Mochizuki, that choosing a
haiku name for people in this group is my job?*

She said she had thought for a long time about what
name might be best for me. She was pleased with my love
of haiku and with my effort. I was a seedling, she told our
haiku group, and she wondered to what parts of the world

I might bring this love of haiku, and what might grow from this seedling.

The name I have chosen for you is composed of two characters—fu, *meaning "not," and* ji, *meaning "two." Not two. Fuji. It is a homonym for Mount Fuji, which is fitting, as this haiku group meets in the foothills of Mount Fuji. But I also hope it reminds you that you are like no other and that you must write haiku that reflect who you are.*

I had hoped to receive a beautiful haiku name, something with the Chinese characters for "snow" or "moon" or "flower." But Momoko was right. A haiku, she had once said, is a piece of one's soul. My new name was a reminder to me that haiku is not just about writing about beauty, but is a path of self-discovery. I could not expect to write good haiku if I was not seeking to be true to myself. The name Momoko gave me would inspire me within, down that narrow road, to the interior.

ENDNOTES

CHAPTER 1: THE MAN FROM HIROSHIMA

[1] Many haiku poets use a *haigo,* or haiku name, in place of their given name. Haiku poets are referred to by these haiku names, rather than by their family names. So, for instance, Masaoka Shiki is known as Shiki, and Yosa Buson is commonly referred to as Buson.

CHAPTER 3: DUCKS IN THE PALACE MOAT

[2] The haiku translation is my own, but is similar to R. H. Blyth, *Haiku,* vol. 3 (Summer/Autumn) (Tokyo: Hokuseido Press, 1982), p. 876.

[3] Muneta Yasumasa, ed., *Kigo hayabiki jiten* (Tokyo: Gakken Press, 2000), p. 62.

CHAPTER 6: FOG ON THE LAKE

[4] John Dower, *Embracing Defeat: Japan in the Wake of World War II* (New York: W. W. Norton/The New Press, 1999), p. 310. It is from the daughter of R. H. Blyth, Harumi Blyth, that I learned that her father worked on his seminal four-volume treatise on Japanese haiku while interned in Japan during World War II.

[5] R. H. Blyth, *Haiku,* vol. 1 (Eastern Culture), (Tokyo: Hokuseido Press, 1981), p. 5.

[6] *Bashō: Narrow Road to the Deep North and Other Travel Sketches,* trans. Nobuyuki Yuasa (London: Penguin Books, 1966), p. 27.

[7]　R. H. Blyth, *A History of Haiku*, vol. 1 (Tokyo: Hokuseido Press, 1963), p. 110.

[8]　The translations of this haiku and annotated passage are from *Bashō: Narrow Road to the Deep North and Other Travel Sketches*, p. 52.

[9]　The translation of this annotated passage is from Seishi Yamaguchi, *The Essence of Modern Haiku: 300 Poems by Seishi Yamaguchi*, trans. Takashi Kodaira and Alfred H. Marks (Atlanta, GA: Mangajin, 1993), p. 243.

[10]　Originally published in Japanese in Sōjin Furutachi, ed., *Yamaguchi Seison-shū*, Kyakuchū meiku series 1, vol. 20 (Tokyo: Haijin Kyōkai, 1989), p. 134.

[11]　Ibid., p. 154.

[12]　The translations of this haiku and annotated passage are from Makoto Ōoka, *Oriori no Uta: Poems for All Seasons*, trans. Janine Beichman (Tokyo: Kodansha International, Bilingual Books, 2000), p. 71.

CHAPTER 7: WHITE LEEKS

[13]　For more on Yanagi Sōetsu and the *mingei* movement, see Japan Folk Crafts Museum, *Mingei: Masterpieces of Japanese Folkcraft* (Tokyo: Kodansha International, 1991).

CHAPTER 8: THE GRAPEVINE TRELLIS

[14]　The *daikon* is a large white Japanese radish.

CHAPTER 11: MR. FUKATSU'S BASHŌ

[15] The haiku translation is my own, but is similar to Robert Hass, ed. and trans., *The Essential Haiku: Versions of Bashō, Buson, and Issa* (Hopewell, NJ: Ecco Press, 1994), p. 42.

CHAPTER 12: CHERRY BLOSSOMS

[16] Makoto Ōoka, *The Poetry and Poetics of Ancient Japan*, trans. Thomas Fitzsimmons (Santa Fe, NM: Katydid Books, 1997), p. 21.

[17] The translation of this poem is from Geoffrey Bownas and Anthony Thwaite, eds., *The Penguin Book of Japanese Verse* (Baltimore: Penguin Books, 1970).

CHAPTER 13: WITHERED FIELDS

[18] A *shōji* is a sliding screen covered with white Japanese paper.

[19] The translations of these poems are from *Masaoka Shiki: Selected Poems*, trans. Burton Watson (New York: Columbia University Press, 1997), pp. 57–59.

WRITING HAIKU IN ENGLISH

When I left Japan, my desire to write haiku followed me. The problem I faced back in America, however, was that I had no idea which of the haiku rules I had learned in Japan applied to English-language haiku. Should I be writing seventeen-syllable, "five-seven-five" haiku, as is common in Japan? I knew that this rhythm was natural in Japanese, but that it was much less natural in English. If I did not write seventeen-syllable haiku, what structure was appropriate? In Japanese, haiku are usually written in a single line, but I noticed that in English many are broken into three lines. And what about "cut-words," which exist only in Japanese? Should I divide images in my haiku using a dash or another marker? And what of seasonal words, so essential to Japanese haiku?

I also struggled with the kinds of subjects I might write about. I had bamboo growing in my backyard in Maryland, and for the first few weeks after my return, I wrote many haiku about bamboo. But when I would take a walk in my neighborhood, I was inspired by the fire hydrants on every block, the blue mailbox down at the corner, and the yellow school bus rumbling past me. I wanted to write haiku about these too.

After some research, I began to see that much of the challenge and excitement of writing haiku in the West comes from the fact that there are no commonly agreed-upon rules. (This is not so far removed from the situation in Japan. There, contemporary poets are challenging the existing haiku rules; in the West, we are struggling to create them.)

Some of the best contemporary North American haiku poets are writing about matters having little or nothing to do with the seasons or nature:

> Alzheimer's ward
> again Father counts
> the afghan squares
> PAMELA MILLER NESS

> I send a fax
> protesting the bombing:
> pages come out hot
> RUTH YARROW

> night after the march
> reading the million-man pledge
> to my pregnant wife
> LENARD D. MOORE

Others are writing beautiful haiku without feeling tied at all to a three-line structure:

> gunshot the length of the lake
> JIM KACIAN

all the clocks in the boxes say it's ten after ten

CHRIS GORDON

Many scholars and poets of haiku have sought to help writers of English-language haiku by proposing definitions. Some years ago, in his seminal work, *The Haiku Handbook*, William J. Higginson suggested the creation of a traditional form for haiku that might involve a roughly twelve-syllable structure. (See William J. Higginson, *The Haiku Handbook: How to Write, Share, and Teach Haiku* [Tokyo: Kodansha International, 1985], pp. 105–6.) Others are defining haiku more in terms of the content than the structure. After years of defining haiku as "usually written in three lines of five, seven, and five syllables," the Haiku Society of America (HSA) changed its definition in 2004 to reflect some of the variety of English-language haiku. The HSA definition, given on the society's web site at www.hsa-haiku.org, now states:

> A haiku is a short poem that uses imagistic language to convey the essence of an experience of nature or the season intuitively linked to the human condition.

But even while offering a new haiku definition, the HSA emphasizes that a definition is "neither a lesson nor instruction for writing." Definitions are meant to be helpful, not constraining. Haiku poet and author Jane Reichhold takes this same approach and, at www.ahapoetry.com/haidefjr.htm, encourages haiku poets to write in a way that makes sense to them: "Make rules for yourself and follow them exactly, or break them completely, outgrow them and find new ones. We are all students and no one 'really' knows how to write a haiku."

My suggestion for readers new to haiku is to start simply by writing what you think is haiku. If you wait until you have a strong sense of what a haiku is before writing, you may be waiting a long time, particularly since the form in English is evolving. Write, and above all read as many good haiku as you can. While you are doing so, read up on what others have to say about haiku. All of this will help you better understand haiku and give you a surer sense of the kind of haiku you want to write.

STARTING YOUR OWN HAIKU GROUP

Starting a haiku group is simple. You will want to think about whom to invite—whether to limit participation to a few friends, or open it to anyone who is interested. You will need to choose a time and location, send out flyers or an email, or just make some telephone calls, and then wait for everyone to show up.

One of the most important questions you will face, as you start making your plans, is what to do when your haiku group meets—how do you wish to run your group?

There is no single, "correct" way to run a haiku group. This is as true in Japan as it is in the rest of the world. Haiku groups vary in terms of how often they meet, the number of participants, whether a haiku theme to write about is specified each month, how many haiku are submitted at each meeting, and, particularly in North America, how much feedback is given.

The format I offer below is drawn from advice I received from haiku poets in North America and Japan, and my own experience starting a haiku group in Quebec City. No two haiku groups are alike, as a group will reflect the personalities and desires of its members. Yours might, for instance, start with the format I suggest below and then evolve into something that better fits the needs of your members. If so, I can only applaud you.

For a group in which many participants are new to haiku, I recommend meeting once a month and setting a target of only three haiku contributions a month. A core of about six participants will help keep the group going, although it is nice to have at least ten members at each session, since the more members you have, the more haiku you will be reading.

In a traditional, Japanese-style haiku group meeting (*kukai* in Japanese), participants silently contemplate haiku and share their haiku with others. A *kukai* can help motivate you to produce haiku regularly, set aside time to consider the world around you, and give you insight into your own writing. That said, many haiku poets, especially those who are new to the field, may want to bolster the *kukai* experience with more directed learning. For this reason, I suggest a two-part structure for your meetings. The first part is modeled on a traditional Japanese *kukai*. There is no discussion, simply quiet contemplation of haiku, followed by the reading aloud of each person's favorite three haiku. (This part might take anywhere from forty-five minutes to an hour and a half, depending on the size of the group.) The second part of the meeting focuses on learning more about haiku. The topic and format of the second part of each meeting might vary from month to month, depending on the interests of the group. It is a good idea to take a break between the quiet, contemplative session and the second part, which is more interactive.

PART I: THE *KUKAI*, OR CONTEMPLATIVE MEETING

In a traditional Japanese *kukai*, each participant writes haiku, brings them to the meeting, and submits them anonymously for selection. Learning takes place over time, in the contemplation of haiku and in seeing which haiku are selected. If a haiku master is present, the master will give brief feedback at the end of the session (just as Momoko did in this book).

Your group will need 3x5 index cards and letter-size paper in two different colors (yellow and blue, for the purpose of this example). Follow these steps:

1. At the beginning of the session, hand out three index cards, one sheet of yellow paper, and one sheet of blue paper to each participant.

2. Ask participants to write down their haiku on the index cards, one haiku to a card, and place the cards face down in the middle of a table. Tell them that they should not write their names on these cards.

3. When all the cards are in the center, have someone shuffle the cards and deal them out, three to a person.

4. Write down, on a single sheet of yellow paper, the three haiku you have been handed.

5. Going around the room, count off aloud, so that each person has a number, starting with one. Write down your number in the upper right-hand corner of the yellow sheet.

6. Now, for the next forty-five minutes to an hour (depending on the size of the group), enjoy reading *in silence* all of the haiku on the yellow sheets of paper,

as they are slowly passed around the room from right to left. Read a page, and when you have finished contemplating it, pass it to the left. (Don't worry if the sheets start piling up or if you read more quickly than your neighbor. Eventually, all the papers will make their way around the room, and you will be back with your originally numbered yellow page.)

7. While you are peacefully reading these sheets, jot down those you particularly enjoy on your blue sheet of paper. After reading and contemplating all of the poems that have gone around the room, you may have jotted down a dozen or more haiku. Circle your three favorite haiku.

8. Beginning with the person who has the sheet marked number one, each participant will read aloud his or her three favorite haiku. After reading a haiku aloud, pause so that the author of the haiku can announce his or her name. Do nothing more than read aloud the haiku you enjoyed! (Resist the temptation to change your selection simply because a haiku has already been chosen several times.) While some haiku groups do offer feedback at this point, I have found that unless a basis of trust already exists among all group members, it may be best to let the author seek feedback individually during the break, or at another time.

9. After everyone has had a chance to read aloud his or her three favorites, the contemplative part of the

kukai is over. In Japan, it is at this point that a haiku master, if present, will comment briefly on a number of haiku. Unless your group agrees in advance to have someone offer feedback, I recommend that feedback not be given. (You will be surprised at how much more eager people are to give feedback than to receive it.) In some Japanese *kukai* where a haiku master is not present, the group will ask the poets whose haiku received the most votes to talk a bit about their haiku. I have used this system and found that it works quite well.

A few additional thoughts:

- You may want to keep the format of the *kukai* part of your meeting unchanged from month to month, as the routine helps participants concentrate on writing haiku and minimizes the stress of sharing their haiku with others.

- For the first meeting of your haiku group, not everyone will come with three haiku in hand (especially if your group consists largely of newcomers to haiku). In this case, and only for a person's first meeting, you may wish to have on hand some haiku written by well-known haiku poets. The new member can then "adopt" the profile of the well-known poet for the evening and submit these haiku, with the understanding that when these haiku are chosen, the beginner announces the name of the actual author. This will at least allow new members to get a feel for how the *kukai* unfolds. The next time, they can bring their own haiku.

• If your group consists largely of people new to haiku, you may wish at the end of the first session to hand out a few sheets with haiku written by well-known haiku poets, along with the names of the poets and the sources of publication. This helps the beginner start to explore good haiku.

• At the end of a haiku group meeting, it is a good idea to collect and destroy all of the blue and yellow sheets and index cards used during the session. This helps prevent participants walking out of the meeting with someone else's poem. Even with the best of intentions, it is all too easy after having scrawled dozens of haiku on a piece of paper to lose track of which haiku are ours, and which are the work of others.

PART 2: HAIKU STUDY

Haiku is so common in Japan that it is easy for people to learn more about haiku on their own, between group meetings. In Japan, there are magazines devoted exclusively to haiku, as well as books and even television programs on haiku. Members of a haiku group are often affiliated with a larger organization that has its own magazine, where members can read about haiku and publish their own writing. (Kuroda Momoko, for example, runs the Aoi haiku group, which includes a monthly subscription magazine.)

In the West, it can be more of a challenge for new

haiku poets to learn more about haiku. Also, while enjoying the *kukai* format, many people in the West may also appreciate having a second half of the meeting—after the *kukai* and a short break—in which haiku is studied more directly. This second half of the meeting might run anywhere from a half-hour to an hour.

In the study component, members might wish to take turns being responsible for the session. The person who is responsible for that month's session will choose the topic and either lead or organize the session. Some options to choose from include:

- Make a presentation on a particular poet (this is an excellent task for a beginning haiku poet to take on).

- Organize a workshop on writing haiku. Specific topics might include punctuation, syllables in haiku, line breaks, objectivity versus subjectivity, fine-tuning your haiku.

- Invite a guest haiku poet to give a reading and talk about his or her work.

- Organize a workshop on reading haiku aloud (a skill different from writing haiku).

- Make a presentation on Internet sites dedicated to haiku (hand out a list of recommended web sites).

- Make a presentation on haiku in other parts of the world.

- Research and describe the many haiku contests and how to submit your haiku to a contest.

- Research and describe how and where to submit hai-ku for publication.

Above all, make your haiku group enjoyable. Eating, drinking, and socializing with others who enjoy haiku is an essential aspect of haiku groups. Have fun!

FURTHER READING ON HAIKU

There are a number of quality publications and hundreds of haiku-related web sites that showcase haiku and offer good explanations of various aspects of the art. You will not be lacking in material to read. Here I list only a very few of these books, journals, and web sites to get you started. Some of the best haiku by contemporary poets are being published in journals and small presses, so I encourage you to explore these further.

Two organizations, the Haiku Society of America (www.hsa-haiku.org) and Haiku Canada (www.haiku canada.org), in addition to having useful web sites, produce haiku newsletters and journals and organize haiku gatherings. Members also receive a handy membership list, which can help put you in touch with other haiku poets in your region.

My apologies to the many other wonderful publications and sites that, for space considerations, I was unable to list.

JOURNALS

Acorn
   (journal, edited by A. C. Missias)
ant ant ant ant ant
   (journal, edited by Chris Gordon)

Blithe Spirit
> (journal of the British Haiku Society, edited by Graham High)

bottle rockets
> (journal, edited by Stanford M. Forrester)

Frogpond
> (international membership journal of the Haiku Society of America, currently edited by John Stevenson)

Gong
> (journal of the Association Française de Haiku, edited by Dominique Chipot)

Haiku Canada Newsletter
> (edited by LeRoy Gorman)

The Heron's Nest
> (online journal, edited by Christopher Herold)
> www.theheronsnest.com

Modern Haiku
> (journal, edited by Lee Gurga)

Raw NerVZ
> (journal, edited by Dorothy Howard)

Reeds
> (journal of *haiga*, edited by Jeanne Emrich)

South by Southeast
> (journal, edited by Stephen Addiss)

Tundra
> (journal, edited by Michael Dylan Welch)

Upstate Dim Sum
(print and online journal)
homepage.mac.com/gnach/upds%20folder/upds/

WEB SITES AND INTERNET JOURNALS

Aha!Poetry
www.ahapoetry.com

Brooks Books Haiku
www.brooksbookshaiku.com

Haiku Hut
www.haikuhut.com

Haiku Hut Poetry Forums
www.poetrylives.com/HaikuHut

Haikuworld
www.haikuworld.org

Nick Virgilio Poetry Project
www.nickvirgilio.rutgers.edu/htm/miscellaneous/
misc2.htm

Simply Haiku
www.simplyhaiku.com

Temps Libres/Free Times
www.tempslibres.org/

World Haiku Association
www.worldhaiku.net/

World Haiku Club
www.worldhaikuclub.org

World Haiku Review
www.worldhaikureview.org

A listing of more haiku-related web sites can be found at:
www.dmoz.org/Arts/Literature/Poetry/Forms/Haiku_
and_Related_Forms

A SAMPLING OF BOOKS

Barlow, John, and Martin Lucas. *The New Haiku.* Liverpool: Snapshot Press, 2002.

Blyth, R. H. *Haiku.* 4 volumes. Tokyo: Hokuseido Press, 1949–52.

Brandi, John, and Dennis Maloney. *The Unswept Path: Contemporary American Haiku.* Buffalo, NY: White Pine Press, 2005.

Kacian, Jim, ed. *The Red Moon Anthology of English Language Haiku.* Winchester, VA: Red Moon Press, 1996–.

Ross, Bruce. *Haiku Moment: An Anthology of Contemporary North American Haiku.* Rutland, VT, and Tokyo: Charles E. Tuttle Company, 1993.

Van Den Heuvel, Cor, ed. *The Haiku Anthology: Haiku and Senryu in English.* Revised edition. New York: Simon and Schuster, 1986.

Wright, Richard. *Haiku: This Other World.* Edited by Yoshinobu Hakutani and Robert L. Tener. New York: Anchor Books, 2000.

QUESTIONS FOR READING GROUPS

1. What has your experience with poetry been to this point? Has there been a particular poet whose work you enjoyed? Have you had a favorite poem?

2. Have you ever tried to write poetry? At what point in your life did you do this? What was the experience like?

3. The author of this book had many preconceptions about what a poet should be like, and she describes herself as someone who is "not the poetic type." Do you think there is a "poetic type," and how would you describe the type? Has the book challenged your ideas about this type at all?

4. In the book, the author describes some of the ways that she combines writing poetry with her professional life and her home life (for instance, looking words up in her electronic dictionary as she walks around town with her children). What are some examples of the ways that she combines these aspects of her life? Are there any specific new ways that come to mind now in which you might be able to combine your own interest in reading or writing with your professional life or your home life?

5. When talking about world events and her work as a diplomat, the author mentions a number of compet-

ing strategic and human rights concerns. What are they? How would you reconcile these concerns?

6. Why do you think the author is drawn to the world of haiku?

7. What insights did you gain into Japanese culture, society, or language from the book?

CREDITS AND PERMISSIONS

In addition to receiving the permission of Kuroda Momoko to draw from her work, and that of other Japanese poets where appropriate and feasible, I obtained permission from the following authors and publishers for use of their work.

Translation of Bashō's haiku "the ancient poet who pitied . . ." and the paragraph following, from *Bashō: Narrow Road to the Deep North and Other Travel Sketches*, trans. Nobuyuki Yuasa (London: Penguin Books, 1966), p. 52: reprinted by permission of Penguin Books, Ltd.

"When the east wind blows . . ." by Sugawara no Michizane, from Geoffrey Bownas and Anthony Thwaite, eds., *The Penguin Book of Japanese Verse* (Baltimore: Penguin Books, 1970): reprinted by permission of the authors.

"all the clocks" by Chris Gordon, which previously appeared in *Noon*: reprinted by permission of the author.

Seison haiku and annotations by Saitō Kafū and Kuroda Momoko, from Sōjin Furutachi, ed., *Yamaguchi Seison-shū*, Kyakuchū meiku series 1, vol. 20 (Tokyo: Haijin Kyōkai, 1989), pp. 134, 154: reprinted by permission of Saitō Kafū, Kuroda Momoko, and Yamaguchi Seison Estate.

Three haiku by Elizabeth Guinsbourg: reprinted by permission of the author.

"gunshot" by Jim Kacian: reprinted by permission of the author.

"night after the march" by Lenard D. Moore, which previously appeared in *Gathering at the Crossroads* (Winchester, VA: Red Moon Press, 2003): reprinted by permission of the author.

"Alzheimer's ward" by Pamela Miller Ness, which previously appeared in *bottle rockets* 3 (Fall/Winter 2000): reprinted by permission of the author.

Passage and translation of Kijō haiku from Makoto Ōoka, *Oriori no Uta: Poems for All Seasons*, trans. Janine Beichman (Tokyo: Kodansha International, Bilingual Books, 2000), p. 71: reprinted by permission of Kodansha International.

"Sickbed Snowfall: Four Poems by Shiki," from *Masaoka Shiki: Selected Poems,* trans. Burton Watson (New York: Columbia University Press, 1997), pp. 57–59: reprinted by permission of the publisher.

"I send a fax," by Ruth Yarrow: reprinted by permission of the author.

For seasonal references for *kamo* (duck) and for Tezuka Misa haiku, from Muneta Yasumasa, ed., *Kigo hayabiki jiten* (Tokyo: Gakken Press, 2000): reprinted by permission of the publisher and the author, respectively.

Abigail Friedman was born in Washington, D.C. and grew up in Maryland. She joined the Foreign Service in 1988 and has served her country in Washington, Paris, Tokyo, and the Azores, and most recently as Consul General in Quebec City.

Abigail first lived in Japan in 1986–88, when she accompanied her husband, an English teacher, to Hiroshima. She later returned to Japan as a diplomat, serving two tours at the U.S. Embassy in Tokyo, from 1992 to 1995 and from 2000 to 2003. She worked on North Korea issues during her second tour in Tokyo, and in Washington the following year as Asia Bureau Special Assistant and as a member of the U.S. delegation to the Six Party Talks on North Korea.

Earlier in her career, while in the Political Military Bureau, Abigail was detailed to the U.N. to work on post–Gulf War Iraq issues. She served as speechwriter to Walter Mondale, then Ambassador to Japan, from 1994 to 1995. Later she participated in the Dayton Peace negotiations for Bosnia and Herzegovina and was an election observer in Srebrenica, Bosnia and a member of the U.S. delegation to the Rambouillet talks on Kosovo.

Abigail received her B.A. with honors from Harvard University and her J.D. from the Georgetown University Law Center. She speaks French, Japanese, Portuguese, and Spanish. She is married and has three children. She is a member of the Haiku Society of America and Haiku Canada, and is the founder of a haiku group in Quebec City.